THE ANIMATOR'S SURVIVAL KIT™

FLEXIBILITY AND WEIGHT

RICHARD WILLIAMS

DIRECTOR OF ANIMATION 'WHO FRAMED ROGER RABBIT'

FLEXIBILITY AND WEIGHT

THE ANIMATOR'S SURVIVAL KIT™

First published in this edition in 2021
by Faber & Faber Ltd
Bloomsbury House
74–77 Great Russell Street
London WC1B 3DA

Typeset by Faber & Faber Ltd
Printed and bound in India

A CIP record for this book
is available from the British Library

ISBN 978–0–571–35843–4

10 9 8 7 6 5 4 3 2 1

WHEN I PERSUADED the FAMOUS DISNEY PIONEER ANIMATOR ART BABBITT TO GIVE US A MONTH-LONG SERIES OF MASTERCLASSES, IT WAS LIKE DRINKING COOL WATER IN the DESERT.

A BIG EYE-OPENER FOR ME WAS HOW TO GET FROM A TO B IN the MOST INTERESTING WAY.

HOW DO WE LOOSEN THINGS UP and GET SNAP and VITALITY INTO OUR PERFORMANCES at the SAME TIME AS KEEPING the FIGURE STABLE and SOLID?

ART REVEALED ONE OF the GREAT SECRETS OF ANIMATION, WHICH IS—"SUCCESSIVE BREAKING OF JOINTS TO GIVE FLEXIBILITY."

IT'S A MOUTHFUL, BUT ONCE YOU GET the IDEA, the RESULTS ARE MAGIC.

The VERY FIRST THING I ASKED the 'KING' OF ANIMATORS MILT KAHL WAS "HOW DID YOU EVER GET THAT JUNGLE BOOK TIGER TO WEIGH SO MUCH?"

HE SAID, "I KNOW WHERE the WEIGHT IS ON EVERY DRAWING. I KNOW WHERE IT'S COMING FROM and WHERE IT'S JUST TRAVELLING OVER and WHERE the WEIGHT IS TRANSFERRING TO."

THAT'S IT! I'VE FOUND the BEST WAY TO SHOW WEIGHT IS TO BE AWARE OF IT, CONSCIOUS OF IT and TO THINK ABOUT IT ALL the TIME. OTHERWISE YOU CAN END UP WITH A DINOSAUR RUNNING AROUND LIKE A MOUSE.

THERE'S WEIGHT IN EVERYTHING — IT'S NOT JUST PICKING UP A ROCK THAT HAS WEIGHT, EVEN STIRRING A CUP OF TEA HAS WEIGHT.

AS the MAN SAID, "I KNOW WHERE the WEIGHT IS ON EVERY DRAWING."

Richard Williams

FLEXIBILITY

AS I SEE IT, THERE ARE 2 BIG ANIMATION FLAWS —

WE EITHER HAVE The 'KING KONG' EFFECT
WHERE EVERYTHING MOVES AROUND
The SAME AMOUNT

 OR

EVERYTHING IS FLASHING AROUND
ALL OVER The PLACE

 SO

WE WANT TO HAVE A STABLE IMAGE
and STILL HAVE FLEXIBILITY

 AND

THIS IS HOW WE GET IT:

The FOLLOWING DEVICES ARE GUARANTEED TO LIMBER UP, LOOSEN UP and
GIVE 'SNAP' and VITALITY TO OUR PERFORMANCE WHILE KEEPING The FIGURE
STABLE and SOLID.

WE'VE ALREADY INTRODUCED SOME OF THESE DEVICES WITH WALKS and RUNS, BUT I WANT TO TAKE EACH OF THEM SEPARATELY and DIG INTO THEM.

FIRST, (The BREAKDOWN)

A GREAT WAY TO GET FLEXIBILITY IS WHERE WE'RE GOING TO PLACE

The BREAKDOWN DRAWING
OR PASSING POSITION
OR MIDDLE POSITION
OR INTERMEDIATE POSITION
(WHATEVER YOU WANT TO CALL IT)

– BETWEEN 2 EXTREMES.

WHERE DO WE GO IN The MIDDLE? CRUCIAL! AS WE'VE SEEN WITH The WALKS, IT GIVES CHARACTER TO The MOVE. IT'S A TRAVELLER – A TRANSITIONAL POSITION. AND WHERE WE PUT IT IS SO IMPORTANT. IT'S The SECRET OF ANIMATION, I TELL YOU!

IT STOPS THINGS JUST GOING BORINGLY FROM A TO B.
GO SOMEWHERE ELSE THAT'S INTERESTING EN ROUTE FROM A TO B.

EMERY HAWKINS, A MASTER ANIMATOR OF 'CHANGE' SAID TO ME,

"DICK, DON'T GO FROM A TO B.
GO FROM A to X to B.
GO FROM A to G to B.
GO SOMEWHERE ELSE IN The MIDDLE!"

A SIMPLE, POWERFUL TOOL:

I FIRST GOT ONTO THIS BY WORKING WITH KEN HARRIS, WHEN HE'D CUT UP MY DRAWINGS, OR BITS OF THEM, and HE'D STICK THEM DOWN IN A DIFFERENT PLACE.

I ENDED UP FEELING SO STRONGLY ABOUT The BREAKDOWN THAT FOR YEARS I WENT AROUND RANTING and RAVING THAT I COULD WRITE A WHOLE BOOK ABOUT IT. (IT HAS ONLY JUST OCCURRED TO ME THAT THIS IS IT.)

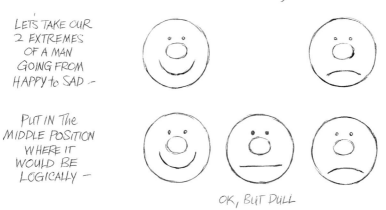

LET'S TAKE OUR
2 EXTREMES
OF A MAN
GOING FROM
HAPPY to SAD –

PUT IN The
MIDDLE POSITION
WHERE IT
WOULD BE
LOGICALLY –

OK, BUT DULL

	EXTREME	BREAKDOWN	EXTREME	

RIGHT, LET'S GO SOMEWHERE ELSE IN THE MIDDLE. = MORE INTEREST. MORE 'CHANGE'

WE COULD EVEN JUST KEEP THE SAME MOUTH and DELAY THE CHANGE - = A QUICKER CHANGE - MORE VITALITY

OR THE CONVERSE - ADVANCE THE CHANGE = A QUICKER UNHAPPINESS.

LET'S KEEP THE SAME MOUTH BUT PUSH IT UP - = IT WOULD AFFECT THE CHEEKS and MAYBE THE EYES AND GIVE MORE CHANGE TO UNHAPPY

KEEP THE SAME MOUTH BUT DROP IT DOWN = IT WOULD DISTEND THE FACE STRETCHING THE CHEEKS, NOSE, EYES.

OR TAKE THE UNHAPPY MOUTH and PUSH IT UP - = A TOTALLY DIFFERENT CHANGE

STRAIGHTEN IT and PUSH IT UP.- = GULP...

STRAIGHT and LOWER? = OH, OH...

5

	EXTREME	BREAKDOWN	EXTREME		
DO WE GO UP ON ONE SIDE?				=	THINKS ABOUT IT.
INCREASE the SMILE?				=	FALSE CONFIDENCE
REDUCE IT?				=	HMMM....
LET'S REDUCE the UNHAPPY MOUTH				=	I KNEW IT...
EVEN JUST A SIMPLE BLINK				=	GIVES SOME MOBILITY
WE CAN START TO STRETCH THINGS				=	OOPS.
LET'S START TO BE IMAGINATIVE..				=	SOMETHING I ET? OR HAD A DRINK?
				=	YOUR SECRET IS SAFE WITH ME

EXTREME   BREAKDOWN   EXTREME

WE CAN GO
ON LIKE THIS
FOREVER...

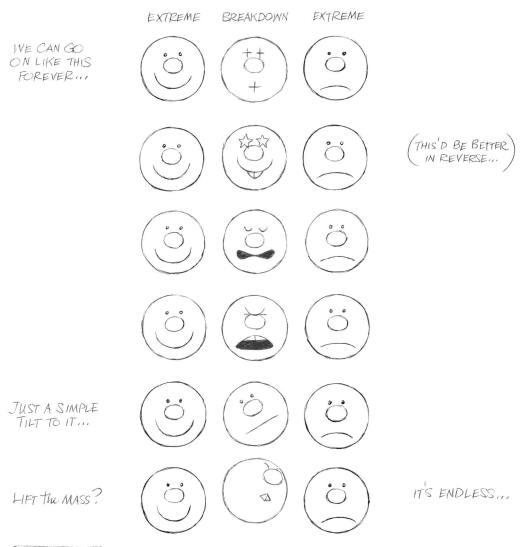

(THIS'D BE BETTER
IN REVERSE...)

JUST A SIMPLE
TILT TO IT...

LIFT The MASS?

IT'S ENDLESS...

(CONCLUSION:)

WHERE WE GO WITH The MIDDLE 'TRAVELLING' POSITION
HAS A PROFOUND EFFECT ON The ACTION and CHARACTER.

I HANG MY HAT ON THIS!

MAKE The EXTREMES (OR CONTACTS) THEN The BREAKDOWN (OR
PASSING POSITION.) THEN MAKE The NEXT BREAKDOWN BETWEEN
The EXTREME and The MAIN BREAKDOWN. KEEP BREAKING IT
DOWN INTO EVER SMALLER BITS.
(THEN DO SEPARATE 'STRAIGHT-AHEAD' RUNS ON SEPARATE BITS)

30 YEARS AGO WHEN I WAS FIRST CATCHING ON TO ALL THIS STUFF, I WORKED BRIEFLY WITH ABE LEVITOW, KEN HARRIS'S EARLY PROTEGÉ. ABE DREW BEAUTIFULLY and I WAS IMPRESSED BY BOTH the QUALITY AND the QUANTITY OF HIS WORK. 'FAST AND GOOD'. WORKING ON TOUGH STUFF, ABE PRODUCED 20 to 25 SECONDS A WEEK WHILE the OTHERS MANAGED TO STRUGGLE THROUGH 5 SECONDS. AND ABE'S WAS BETTER.

I ALWAYS REMEMBER ABE SAYING TO ME ON A TUESDAY:

"DICK, I'VE DONE ALL the EXTREMES.
TOMORROW I'M GOING TO BREAK THEM ALL DOWN.
THEN the REST OF the WEEK I'LL ADD IN the BITS and PIECES."

AGAIN,

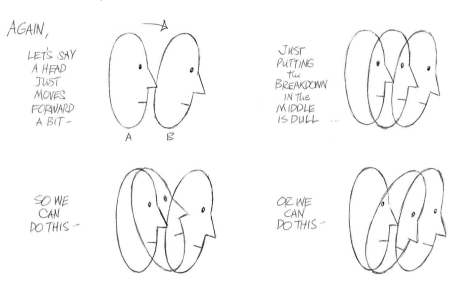

LET'S SAY A HEAD JUST MOVES FORWARD A BIT —

JUST PUTTING the BREAKDOWN IN the MIDDLE IS DULL —

SO WE CAN DO THIS —

OR WE CAN DO THIS —

THIS 'SIMPLE OVERLAP' GIVES US ACTION WITHIN AN ACTION. MORE 'CHANGE' – MORE LIFE.

THIS IS the RAW IDEA.
WE CAN DO IT VERY SUBTLY

OR WE CAN DO IT BROADLY

GIVES US 'MORE BANG FOR OUR BUCK'

— GIVES US MOVEMENT WITHIN A MOVEMENT.

PULLED APART —

AGAIN, GOING FROM HERE TO HERE —

  OR

8

KEN HARRIS WOULD OFTEN DO A VERY INTERESTING THING:

THOUGH HE WAS VERY CONFIDENT OF HIS
ANIMATION ABILITIES, KEN HAD LESS
CONFIDENCE IN HIS DRAWING.

HE LIKED TO MAKE FULL USE OF THE
ROUGH SKETCHES BY CHUCK JONES, HIS
DIRECTOR AT WARNER'S - and LATER ON,
MY DIRECTING DRAWINGS.

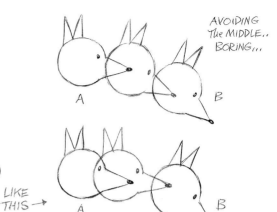

AVOIDING
The MIDDLE..
BORING...

I'D OFTEN FIND KEN MAKING AN EXACT
TRACING OF MY DRAWING "A" OR "B" and USING
IT AS THE PASSING POSITION - (OR BREAKDOWN)

BUT HE'D PLACE IT TO FAVOUR DRAWING "A" LIKE
THIS →

OR HE'D PLACE IT TO FAVOUR DRAWING "B" LIKE
THIS →

FAR FROM BEING A LIMITATION, THIS
ACTUALLY WAS AN ASSET TO KEN. IT GAVE
HIS WORK A STABILITY - INSTEAD OF HAVING
FACILE DRAWINGS FLASHING AROUND ALL
OVER THE PLACE - 'OVERANIMATING'.

WATCHING HIM DO THIS - and SEEING the RESULTS, I GRADUALLY LEARNED
TO UNDERSTATE and GET SUBTLE MOVEMENT WHICH WAS STILL 'LIMBER'.

(SIMPLE OVERLAP)

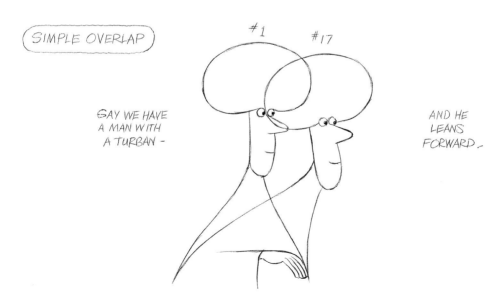

#1   #17

SAY WE HAVE
A MAN WITH
A TURBAN -

AND HE
LEANS
FORWARD -

IF WE TILT the HEAD #9
IN the MIDDLE - and
MAKE IT CLOSER TO #1

WE GET THIS
WITH the HEAD -
and LOOK WHAT HAPPENS
TO the TURBAN MASS -
IT'S SMACK IN the MIDDLE.

THIS CREATES
A REALLY NICE
OVERLAPPING
OF the MASSES
ON A VERY
SIMPLE MOVE -

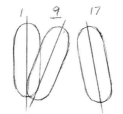

and WE'VE USED
ONLY 3 POSITIONS.
The REST WOULD BE
STRAIGHT
IN BETWEENS.

WE'VE DONE THIS ON A BLAND DESIGN OF A SIMPLE CHARACTER - WITH NO CHANGE
OF EXPRESSION - NOT EVEN A BLINK - MAKING A VERY ORDINARY MOVE.
AND YET IT WILL HAVE A LOT OF LIFE JUST BECAUSE OF the SPACING.

(SO) WE LOOK FOR WAYS TO PLACE the MIDDLE BREAKDOWN POSITION -
(OR POSITIONS) WHERE WE CAN GET AN OVERLAP OF the MASSES.
= MOVEMENT WITHIN MOVEMENT.

4 DRAWING OVERLAP ON A CALIFORNIA - ISSUE MOUSE

A

B

SAME HEAD and BODY
PROGRESSED FORWARD

C

CONTINUES FORWARD the
SAME AMOUNT TILTED DOWN

D

PULLS BACK TILTING DOWN
JUST A BIT MORE.

OF COURSE, THIS BREAKDOWN POSITION KIND OF THING CAN GET OUT OF HAND.
LIKE EVERYTHING ELSE, IT'S HOW, WHEN and WHERE WE USE IT.

WHEN I WAS ASSISTING KEN
HARRIS and THERE'D BE A HAND
SETTLING LIKE THIS -

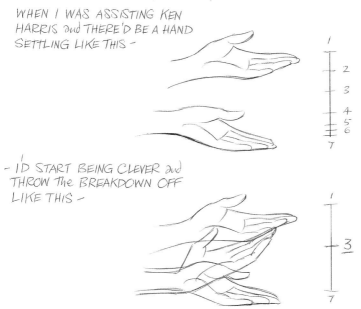

- I'D START BEING CLEVER and
THROW THE BREAKDOWN OFF
LIKE THIS -

KEN WOULD FREAK OUT, "GODDAMN IT, DICK, I JUST WANT A STRAIGHT INBETWEEN
IN THERE! JUST GIVE ME A STRAIGHT INBETWEEN! THE GUY JUST RELAXES HIS HAND!
I DON'T WANT ALL THIS CRAZY FLASHING AROUND ALL OVER THE PLACE KIND OF STUFF!"
(KEN HAD AWFULLY GOOD TASTE.)

BUT WHEN I DID GET TO KNOW HOW, WHEN and WHERE TO USE IT, I CAN ALMOST
SAY I MADE MY LIVING WITH THE BREAKDOWN DRAWING.

I OFTEN HAD TO PRODUCE MASSIVE AMOUNTS OF FOOTAGE AT THE LAST MINUTE.
I BECAME 'THE TELEPHONE ANIMATOR' ANIMATING AT THE SAME TIME AS DOING
THE BUSINESS ON THE PHONE. CLIENTS WOULD RANT, "WE CAME TO YOU BECAUSE
OF HIGH STANDARDS - WE DON'T CARE IF YOUR MAN'S IN THE HOSPITAL OR IN
TIMBUKTOO - IT'S YOUR SHINGLE ON THE DOOR, BUSTER, - YOU FIX IT!"

WE USUALLY HAD GOOD STORYTELLING KEYS and EXTREMES, SO ALL I HAD TO DO
WAS JOIN A LOT OF STUFF UP IN AN INTERESTING WAY. I FOUND THAT ALMOST
ANYTHING WILL WORK. PUT IT SOMEWHERE ELSE IN THE MIDDLE, FAIRLY
INTELLIGENTLY. IT NEVER LET ME DOWN.

OF COURSE, THE WORK WOULDN'T BE AS GOOD AS IF I'D HAD THE TIME TO ANALYSE
and THINK WHAT THE HELL I WAS DOING, BUT AT 5 IN THE MORNING, WITH JET LAG,
HOLDING THE LAB BATH and A GRUMPY CLIENT PHONING IN 4 HOURS, IT GETS YOU THROUGH.

11

NOW WE COME TO A DIFFERENT THING WITH A SIMILAR NAME —

OVERLAPPING ACTION

THIS IS WHERE THINGS MOVE IN PARTS.
— WHERE EVERYTHING DOES NOT HAPPEN AT The SAME TIME.

TAKE A HOLLYWOOD BULLDOG TURNING
QUICKLY AROUND TO SEE SOMETHING —

HIS JOWLS WILL
DRAG AS HE
TURNS

HIS HEAD ARRIVES
AT ITS
DESTINATION

BUT HIS JOWLS and EARS
ARRIVE LATE
and KEEP ON GOING.

THEN SETTLE
DOWN TO NORMAL
(MOUTH MIGHT KEEP ON
GOING — EARS MIGHT
WIGGLE)

THE JARGON IS — "The JOWLS and EARS "DRAG"
and THEN THEY "FOLLOW THROUGH"

THEY'RE The RESULT OF The MAIN ACTION
— GENERATED BY the MAIN ACTION.

'OVERLAPPING ACTION' MEANS ONE PART STARTS FIRST and OTHER PARTS FOLLOW.

LET'S TAKE A TYPICAL UTTERLY BLAND, BORING DESIGN LIKE THEY HAD FOR TV COMMERCIALS
IN The 1950's.—

THIS DULL
CREATURE
IS GOING
TO TURN
and FACE US.

NOT MUCH
TO WORK
WITH
— IS IT ?

WE COULD CONTRIBUTE TO THE BOREDOM BY PUTTING IN AN EQUALLY DULL BREAKDOWN
RIGHT IN THE MIDDLE and GO HOME,

AS MILT KAHL SAID, "THE MOST DIFFICULT THING TO DO IN ANIMATION IS NOTHING.
— YOU KNOW, THATS A VERY TRUE STATEMENT. "

RIGHT, BUT HERE'S HOW WE CAN MAKE 'NOTHING' AT LEAST INTERESTING...
WE CAN TAKE THE CURSE OFF THIS VERY ORDINARY BIT OF ACTION
BY SIMPLY BREAKING THE ACTION INTO PARTS.

PASS POS.

THE EYES WOULD
PROBABLY MOVE
FIRST, BUT WE'RE
STUCK WITH DOTS—

SO LET'S SIMPLY MOVE
THE FOOT FIRST

DELAY THE HEAD
and THE REST

THEN LET'S MOVE THE
STOMACH and HIPS,
STILL DELAY THE HEAD
BUT THROW IN A BLINK

THEN EVERYTHING
SETTLES
and THE HEAD
FOLLOWS LAST.

 SINCE MOST OF OUR BODY ACTIONS START FROM THE HIPS ...

PASS POS

WE'LL MOVE THE HIPS and
STOMACH
FIRST.

TAKES A STEP.
STILL DELAY
THE HEAD.

OTHER FOOT SLIDES
OVER WHILE HEAD IS
IN MID TURN.
THROW IN A SLOW
BLINK.

SETTLES.

WE HAVEN'T EVEN TILTED HIS HEAD OR CHANGED HIS EXPRESSION – BUT SIMPLY BY OVERLAPPING PARTS WE'VE INJECTED LIFE INTO A PEDESTRIAN SITUATION.

PASS POS.

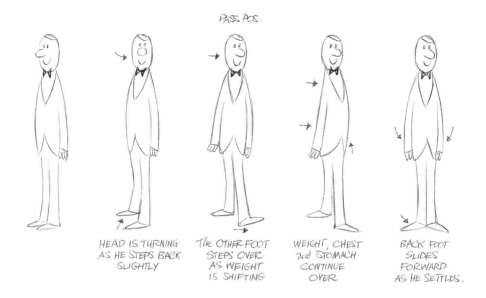

HEAD IS TURNING AS HE STEPS BACK SLIGHTLY

THE OTHER FOOT STEPS OVER AS WEIGHT IS SHIFTING

WEIGHT, CHEST and STOMACH CONTINUE OVER

BACK FOOT SLIDES FORWARD AS HE SETTLES.

WE CAN GO ON LIKE THIS FOREVER...

PASS POS.

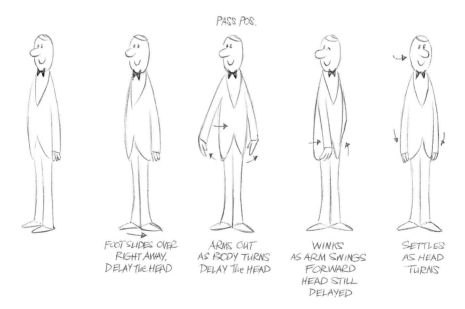

FOOT SLIDES OVER RIGHT AWAY. DELAY THE HEAD

ARMS OUT AS BODY TURNS DELAY THE HEAD

WINKS AS ARM SWINGS FORWARD HEAD STILL DELAYED

SETTLES AS HEAD TURNS

NO MATTER HOW DEADLY THE ACTION IS THAT'S CALLED FOR - WE CAN MAKE IT
MORE INTERESTING BY OVERLAPPING -

PASS POS.

LET'S TURN THE
HEAD FIRST
AND BLINK HIM

NOW LET'S
MOVE WHAT
SHOULDERS
HE HAS

HIPS FOLLOW
THE SHOULDERS
AS HE STEPS

SLIDES OTHER
FOOT SLIGHTLY
AND SETTLES

JUST ONE LITTLE DETAIL THAT'S DIFFERENT WILL CHANGE EVERYTHING.

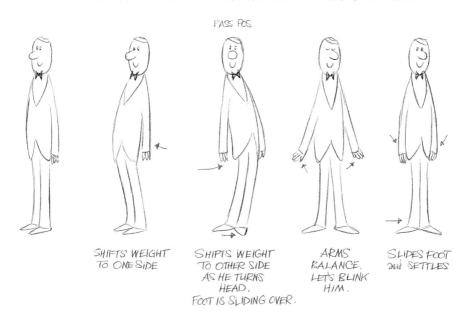

PASS POS

SHIFTS WEIGHT
TO ONE SIDE

SHIFTS WEIGHT
TO OTHER SIDE
AS HE TURNS
HEAD.
FOOT IS SLIDING OVER.

ARMS
BALANCE.
LET'S BLINK
HIM.

SLIDES FOOT
AND SETTLES

SO TO MAKE EVEN THE DULLEST ACTION OR FIGURE INTERESTING, WE BREAK THE BODY INTO SECTIONS – INTO DIFFERENT ENTITIES and MOVE SECTIONS – ONE AT A TIME, CONSTANTLY OVERLAPPING.

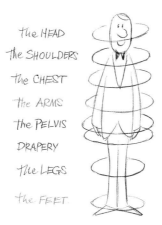

The HEAD
The SHOULDERS
The CHEST
The ARMS
The PELVIS
DRAPERY
The LEGS
The FEET.

AND WE CAN BREAK IT UP INTO EVEN SMALLER SECTIONS IF WE LIKE.

CONCLUSION:

PEOPLE UNFOLD, ONE PART STARTS FIRST, GENERATING THE ENERGY FOR OTHER PARTS TO FOLLOW – WHICH THEN 'FOLLOW THROUGH!' WHEN A FIGURE GOES FROM ONE PLACE TO ANOTHER, A NUMBER OF THINGS TAKE PLACE and EVERYTHING ISN'T HAPPENING AT THE SAME TIME. WE HOLD BACK ON AN ACTION. THINGS DON'T START OR END AT THE SAME TIME. VARIOUS PARTS OF THE BODY OVERLAP EACH OTHER, SO THIS IS WHAT'S CALLED IN THE CRAFT – 'OVERLAPPING ACTION'.

SIMPLE COUNTERACTION

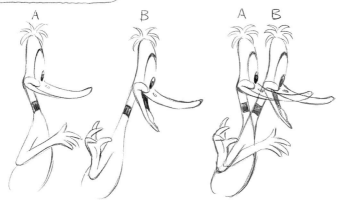

THERE'S NOT MUCH TO SAY ABOUT COUNTERACTION. OBVIOUSLY WE DO IT NATURALLY TO BALANCE OURSELVES.

ONE PART GOES FORWARD AS ANOTHER PART BALANCES BY GOING BACK.

– OR ONE PART GOES UP AS ANOTHER BALANCES BY GOING DOWN.

16

NOW WE COME TO ONE OF The MOST FASCINATING DEVICES IN ANIMATION —

> BREAKING OF JOINTS
> TO GIVE FLEXIBILITY

AND EVEN MORE INTERESTING:

> SUCCESSIVE BREAKING OF
> JOINTS TO GIVE FLEXIBILITY

i.e. WE KEEP ON DOING IT TO LOOSEN THINGS UP.

IT'S QUITE A MOUTHFUL. THE PIONEER DISNEY ANIMATORS DISCOVERED THIS DEVICE and ALL The GOOD GUYS WERE DOING IT, BUT ART BABBITT WAS The ONE WHO GAVE IT A NAME.

WHEN I NOTICED MILT KAHL DOING IT, I REMARKED ON IT, and MILT SAID, "OH, WELL, YOU'VE GOT TO DO THAT." I THINK IF I'D SAID," OH, I NOTICE THAT YOU'RE BREAKING The JOINTS HERE SUCCESSIVELY IN ORDER TO GIVE FLEXIBILITY," HE'D HAVE THROWN ME OUT OF The ROOM.

IT'S NOT WHAT IT'S CALLED — BUT WHAT IS IT?

PUT SIMPLY, IT'S THIS —

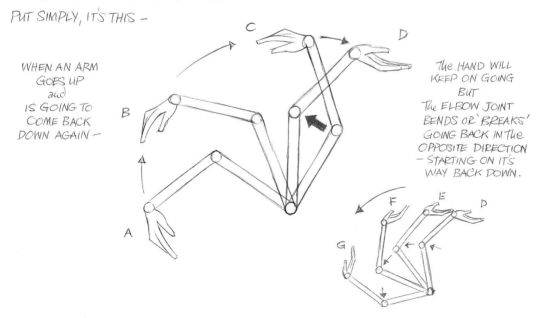

WHEN AN ARM
GOES UP
and
IS GOING TO
COME BACK
DOWN AGAIN —

The HAND WILL
KEEP ON GOING
BUT
The ELBOW JOINT
BENDS OR 'BREAKS'
GOING BACK IN The
OPPOSITE DIRECTION
— STARTING ON IT'S
WAY BACK DOWN.

'BREAKING' MEANS BENDING The JOINT WHETHER OR NOT IT WOULD ACTUALLY BEND IN REALITY.

AND THEN WE'RE GOING TO KEEP ON DOING IT CONTINUOUSLY -'SUCCESSIVELY'- TO MAKE THINGS LIMBER.

GRIM NATWICK, THE FIRST ANIMATOR TO REALLY DRAW WOMEN, ALWAYS SAID,
'CURVES ARE BEAUTIFUL TO WATCH!'

IN THE 1920'S GRIM'S FRIEND, ANIMATOR BILL NOLAN DEVELOPED 'RUBBER HOSE' ANIMATION.
IT WAS NOVEL and FUNNY SINCE NOBODY HAD ANY BONES and EVERYTHING FLOWED WITH
ENDLESS CURVING ACTIONS – LOTS OF VARIATIONS ON FIGURE 8'S, ROUND FIGURES MAKING
ROUNDED ACTIONS.

BUT NOW WE CAN GET CURVES WITH STRAIGHT LINES!

SUCCESSIVE BREAKING JOINTS ENABLE US TO GET THE EFFECT OF CURVED ACTION
BY USING STRAIGHT LINES.
WE'RE FREED FOREVER FROM THE TYRANNY OF HAVING TO ANIMATE RUBBERY FIGURES.
I ALWAYS FIGURED THAT 'DRAWINGS THAT WALK and TALK' SHOULD BE ANY TYPE OF FIGURE
IN ANY STYLE, MADE OF FLESH AND BONES. THIS OPENS UP A PANDORA'S BOX OF STUFF.
WHAT A TOOL! WE CAN HAVE BONES and 'STRAIGHTS' IN OUR FIGURES and STILL HAVE
FLUID, FLOWING MOVEMENT.

SAY WE
IN BETWEEN
THIS ARM
GOING UP -

STRAIGHT
IN BETWEEN
PASS POS

MIGHT
HELP IT BY
DRAGGING
THE HAND -

and
EASE IN
and OUT

IT'S GOING TO BE STIFF AS A BOARD.

IT'S STILL AWFULLY RIGID.

WE WON'T DUCK the PROBLEM WITH A RUBBERISED ARM—

BUT WE'LL BREAK (BEND) the JOINTS STARTING WITH the ELBOW

BREAKDOWN OR PASS POS.

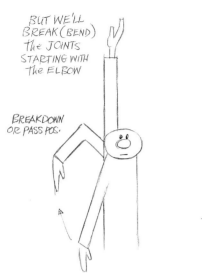

and BREAK IT AGAIN...

The ELBOW ARRIVES FIRST

THIS HAND IS JUST ABOVE →

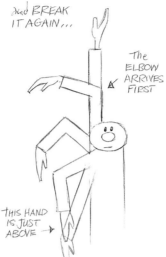

... and BREAK IT AGAIN.

THEN The WRIST ARRIVES BEFORE The HAND

← LOOK WHERE THIS HAND IS.

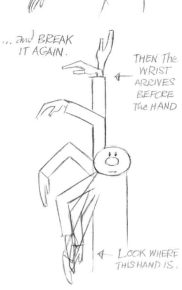

NOW WE GO DOWN The OTHER SIDE – SUCCESSIVELY BREAKING The JOINTS:

PASS POS.

LOOK WHERE THIS ONE IS →

MAKE THIS ONE STRAIGHT BUT DELAY The HAND

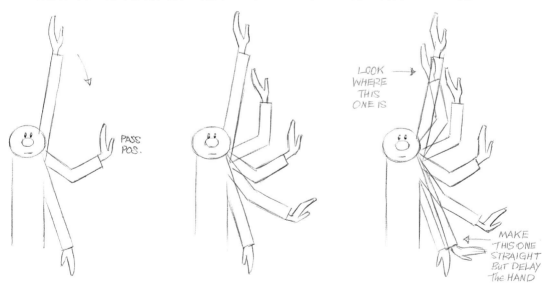

IN THIS EXAMPLE ALL The BENDS OR 'BREAKS' ARE PHYSICALLY POSSIBLE. WE HAVEN'T HAD TO ACTUALLY BEND OR BREAK ANYTHING The WRONG WAY YET.

(BUT WE CAN)

LET'S DO IT AGAIN: THE ELBOW LEADS and THE JOINTS BREAK IN SUCCESSION —

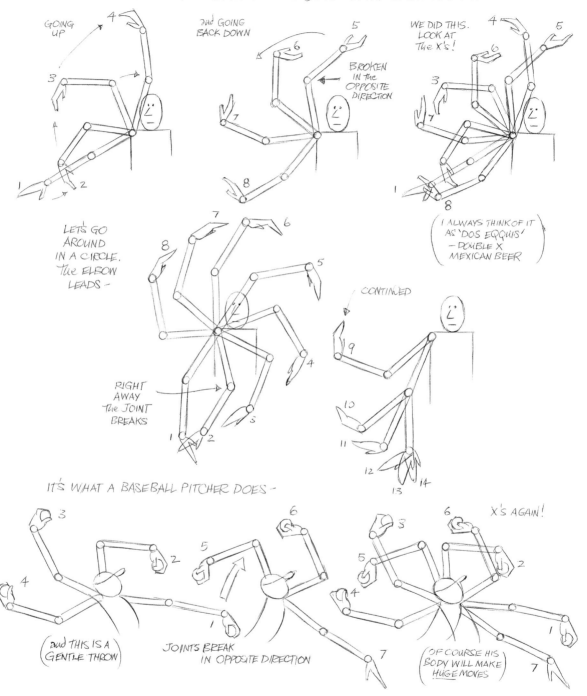

GOING UP

2nd GOING BACK DOWN

WE DID THIS. LOOK AT THE X's!

BROKEN IN THE OPPOSITE DIRECTION

LET'S GO AROUND IN A CIRCLE. THE ELBOW LEADS —

RIGHT AWAY THE JOINT BREAKS

CONTINUED

(I ALWAYS THINK OF IT AS "DOS EQQUIS" — DOUBLE X MEXICAN BEER)

IT'S WHAT A BASEBALL PITCHER DOES —

(and THIS IS A GENTLE THROW)

JOINTS BREAK IN OPPOSITE DIRECTION

X's AGAIN!

(OF COURSE HIS BODY WILL MAKE HUGE MOVES)

20

A THING TO REMEMBER IN BREAKING the JOINTS SUCCESSIVELY IS -
WHERE DOES The ACTION START?
WHAT STARTS MOVING FIRST?
IS IT the ELBOW? The HIPS? The SHOULDER? HEAD?

IN MOST BIG ACTIONS OF The BODY The SOURCE, the START OF The ACTION IS IN The HIPS.

DANCERS SAY "GO FROM YOUR HIPS, LOVE.
FROM The HIPS, DEARIE."

TAKE A MAN SLAPPING A TABLE: The ACTION STARTS FROM HIS HIPS -

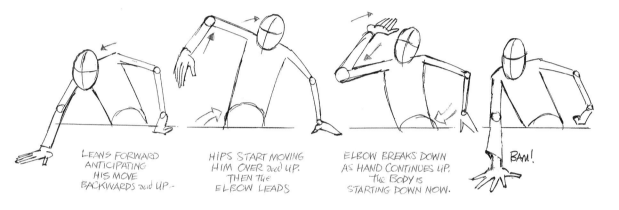

LEANS FORWARD
ANTICIPATING
HIS MOVE
BACKWARDS 2nd UP. -

HIPS START MOVING
HIM OVER 2nd UP.
THEN The
ELBOW LEADS

ELBOW BREAKS DOWN
AS HAND CONTINUES UP,
The BODY IS
STARTING DOWN NOW.

BAM!

WE HAVE LOTS OF LEEWAY TO ACCENTUATE 2nd EXAGGERATE BREAKING JOINTS
BECAUSE IT HAPPENS ALL The TIME IN REALITY.

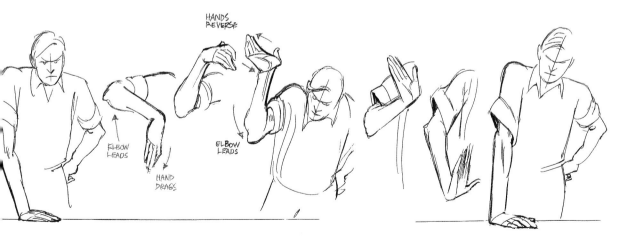

HANDS
REVERSE

ELBOW
LEADS

HAND
DRAGS

ELBOW
LEADS

LET'S KEEP ON HITTING The TABLE -
IT'S AN AWFULLY GOOD EXAMPLE OF HOW WE CAN ACHIEVE The SAME FLEXIBILITY
AS 'RUBBER HOSE' ANIMATION BY BREAKING The JOINTS WHEREVER WE CAN -

GOING UP - The ELBOW LEADS and the HAND DRAGS.

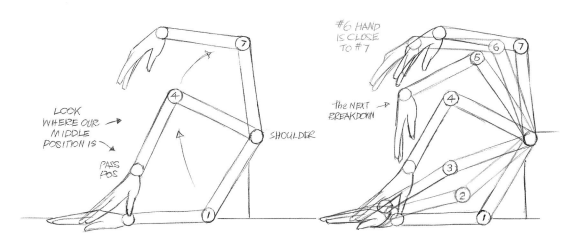

#6 HAND
IS CLOSE
TO #7

LOOK
WHERE OUR
MIDDLE
POSITION IS

the NEXT
BREAKDOWN

SHOULDER

PASS
POS

GOING DOWN - The ELBOW STILL LEADS.

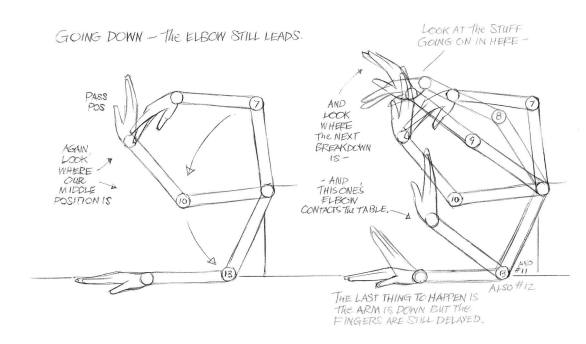

LOOK AT The STUFF
GOING ON IN HERE -

PASS
POS

AGAIN
LOOK
WHERE
OUR
MIDDLE
POSITION IS

AND
LOOK
WHERE
The NEXT
BREAKDOWN
IS -

- AND
THIS ONE'S
ELBOW
CONTACTS The TABLE.

AND
#11

ALSO #12

THE LAST THING TO HAPPEN IS
The ARM IS DOWN BUT The
FINGERS ARE STILL DELAYED.

22

ONE MORE TIME - SHOWING the IDEA SIMPLY.

NOW HE'S GOING TO BANG HIS FIST ON the TABLE -

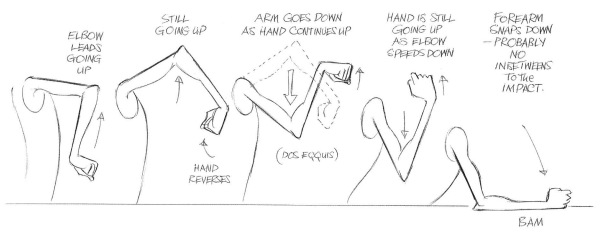

ELBOW LEADS GOING UP

STILL GOING UP

ARM GOES DOWN AS HAND CONTINUES UP

HAND REVERSES

(DOS EQQUIS)

HAND IS STILL GOING UP AS ELBOW SPEEDS DOWN

FOREARM SNAPS DOWN - PROBABLY NO INBETWEENS TO the IMPACT.

BAM

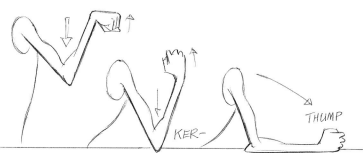

(OR)

AS ON The PRECEEDING PAGE
The ELBOW HITS The TABLE
FIRST -
FOLLOWED BY the FOREARM
and FIST
= MORE UNFOLDING.

KER-

THUMP

IF ALL the JOINTS DO NOT BREAK AT The SAME TIME
WE'LL GET ALL The FLEXIBILITY WE'LL EVER NEED.

IT'S LIKE WHAT WE DO WHEN WE MAKE A PENCIL APPEAR RUBBERY.
AND IT'S JUST WHAT A BALINESE, HINDU OR ORIENTAL TEMPLE DANCER OR A VAUDEVILLE
ECCENTRIC DANCER DOES - AND FRED ASTAIRE! THEY'VE ONLY GOT STRAIGHT BONES
and JOINTS TO WORK WITH - TO GIVE The ILLUSION OF CURVACEOUS, LIMBER MOVEMENT.

BEATING ON A BASS DRUM HAS A VERY SIMILAR ACTION TO SMACKING THE TABLE.

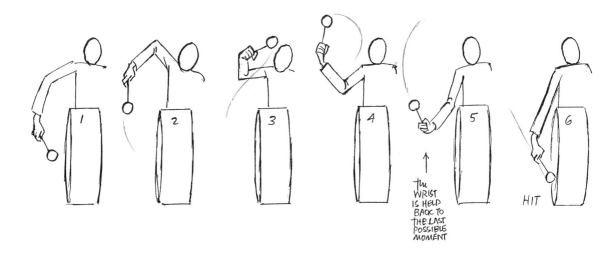

THE WRIST IS HELD BACK TO THE LAST POSSIBLE MOMENT

HIT

THIS BENT JOINT BUSINESS CAN LOOK AWFULLY COMPLICATED AT FIRST BUT YOU QUICKLY GET USED TO IT and USE IT EVERY CHANCE YOU GET. IT BECOMES SECOND NATURE and SIMPLE.

IN 'REALISM' —

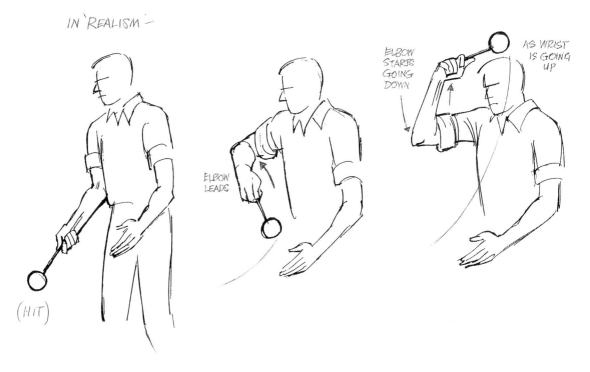

ELBOW STARTS GOING DOWN

AS WRIST IS GOING UP

ELBOW LEADS

(HIT)

OF COURSE, DRUMMERS DO ALL KINDS OF SPINS and FLOURISHES -
BUT THIS IS the BASIC PATTERN -

GOING UP -

COMING DOWN -

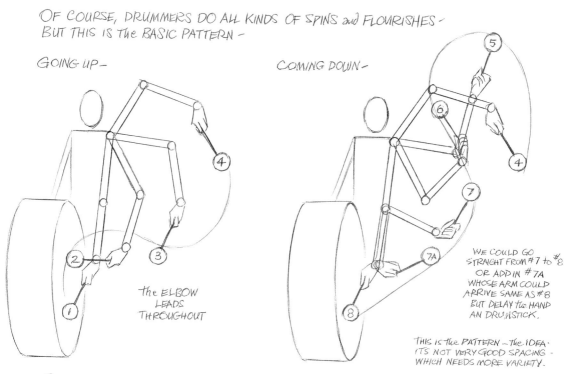

the ELBOW
LEADS
THROUGHOUT

WE COULD GO
STRAIGHT FROM #7 to #8
OR ADD IN #7A
WHOSE ARM COULD
ARRIVE SAME AS #8
BUT DELAY the HAND
AN DRUMSTICK.

THIS IS the PATTERN - the IDEA -
ITS NOT VERY GOOD SPACING -
WHICH NEEDS MORE VARIETY.

RESULT: CURVACEOUS, UNFOLDING MOVEMENT - MADE WITH A RULER.

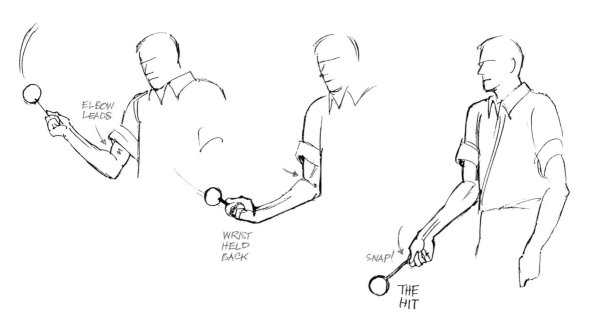

ELBOW
LEADS

WRIST
HELD
BACK

SNAP!

THE
HIT

AN ORCHESTRA CONDUCTOR BREAKS JOINTS IN SUCCESSION LIKE CRAZY.

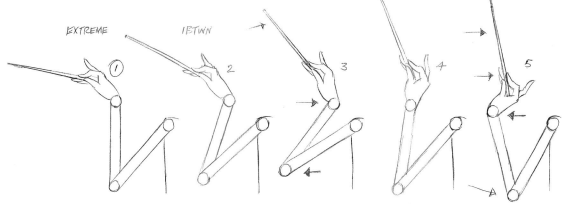

EXTREME   IBTWN

ELBOW GOES FORWARD AS HAND and BATON GO BACK.

WRIST BREAKS FORWARD AS ELBOW, FINGERS, BATON GO BACK

LET'S TAKE the VERY BROAD ACTION OF A MAN SLAPPING OUT A MUSICAL BEAT.—

IBTWN

BAM

(BACK ARCH) REVERSES

IT'S HAPPENING WITH A DOG'S FOOT —

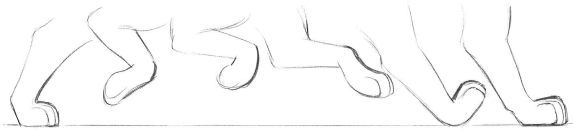

AND THIS IS A REDUCED ACTION FOR A CONDUCTOR...

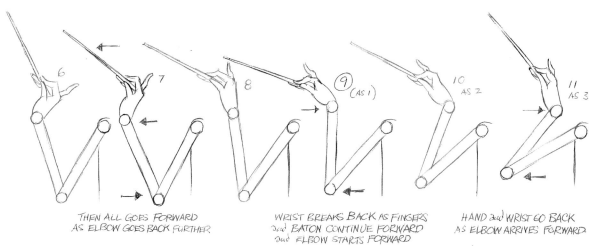

THEN ALL GOES FORWARD
AS ELBOW GOES BACK FURTHER

WRIST BREAKS BACK AS FINGERS
and BATON CONTINUE FORWARD
and ELBOW STARTS FORWARD

HAND and WRIST GO BACK
AS ELBOW ARRIVES FORWARD

IT LOOKS COMPLICATED, BUT WHEN YOU START TO THINK THIS WAY, IT AIN'T.

IT'S BASICALLY THE SAME ACTION AS HITTING
THE TABLE OR BEATING THE BASS DRUM –

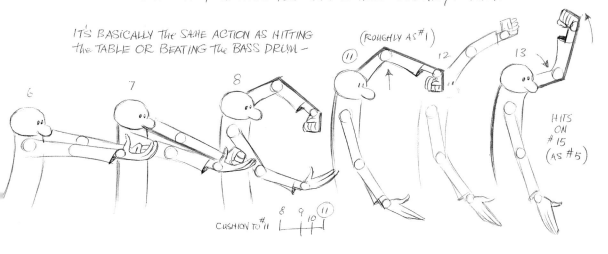

HITS
ON
#15
(AS #5)

OR A FIST BROADLY KNOCKING ON A DOOR –

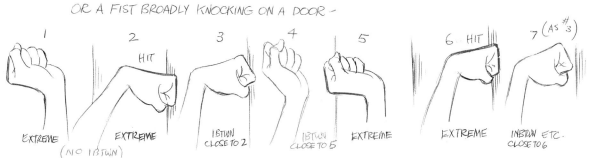

27

THERE ARE LOTS OF SIMPLE LITTLE ACTIONS WHICH CAN BE ENHANCED
WITH JUST A TINY BIT OF FLEXIBILITY.

SAY, A HAND CLAPPING –

 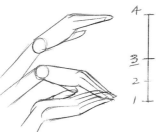 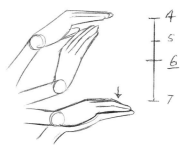

'WRIST LEADS' – TIP DRAGS GOING UP   WRIST LEADS – TIP DRAGS GOING DOWN

ALSO, IT HELPS TO DISPLACE
The PALM SLIGHTLY ON the HIT.
$\left(\dfrac{\text{ON the CONTACT}}{\text{NOT AFTER the HIT}}\right)$,
– DISPLACE The HAND THAT'S
BEING HIT SLIGHTLY.

IF The HAND STAYS IN
The SAME PLACE IT WILL
LACK VITALITY.
WHAT WE FEEL IS The
DISPLACEMENT OF The HIT.

AGAIN, WE COULD DO THIS:

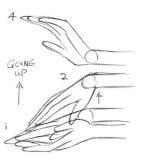 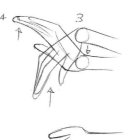  

GOING
UP

BREAKDOWN AS PREVIOUS   The WRIST BREAKS AS   MAYBE HAVE NO   OR COULD HAVE ONE
                           The FINGERS KEEP RISING   IN BETWEEN GOING DOWN   IN BETWEEN GOING DOWN

(OR)

 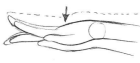 

AND THEN DISPLACE
The PALM ON The HIT.

WITH ONE IN BETWEEN
The WRIST COULD ARRIVE FIRST

OF COURSE, APPLAUSE MAY BE LIKE THIS-
SO WE'D DRAW IT THIS WAY, OBVIOUSLY -

SPANISH FLAMENCO PERSON CLAPS
DIFFERENTLY. TIPS OF FINGERS HIT PALM

AND OBVIOUSLY A WRESTLER CLAPS DIFFERENTLY
FROM A DRUNK OR A DIPLOMAT'S WIFE-OR A BABY.
BUT THE PRINCIPLE IS STILL THIS - A NUMBER OF JOINTS BREAKING, ONE AFTER ANOTHER.

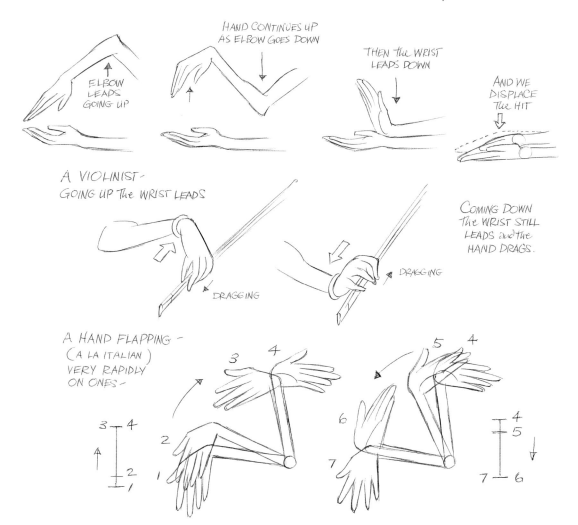

ELBOW LEADS GOING UP

HAND CONTINUES UP
AS ELBOW GOES DOWN

THEN THE WRIST
LEADS DOWN

AND WE
DISPLACE
THE HIT

A VIOLINIST-
GOING UP THE WRIST LEADS

COMING DOWN
THE WRIST STILL
LEADS and THE
HAND DRAGS.

DRAGGING

DRAGGING

A HAND FLAPPING -
(A LA ITALIAN)
VERY RAPIDLY
ON ONES-

29

EVEN IN A LITTLE THING LIKE THIS WE CAN GET FLEXIBILITY —

A   B   C

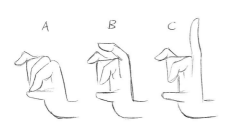

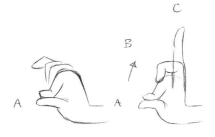

TO OPEN THESE FINGERS A STRAIGHT
INBETWEEN GOING UP WOULD BE OK.

BUT ON THE WAY DOWN
DRAG the INBETWEEN

IF WE HAD A BETTER
FEELING OF CONTACT
and PRESSURE TO BEGIN WITH —

= BETTER GOING UP
WHEN THIS PRESSURE
IS RELEASED.

SAY WE'RE HAMMERING A NAIL —

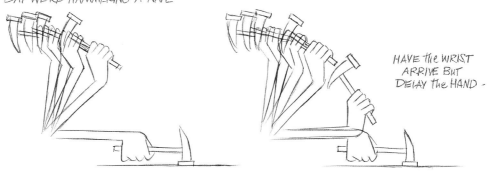

HAVE the WRIST
ARRIVE BUT
DELAY the HAND —

AGAIN, WE CAN TAKE ALL THIS TOO FAR.
BUT the THING IS TO KNOW IT SO WE CAN USE IT WHEN WE WANT (WHICH WILL BE A LOT.)

TAKE SOMEONE'S HANDS
KNOCKING TOGETHER
GOING
'GOODY, GOODY'

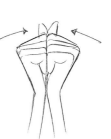

MAYBE WE JUST WANT
TO INBETWEEN IT
FAVOURING
The ANTICIPATE

AND IT
WOULD
BE FINE —

IT MIGHT NOT BE NECESSARY TO 'OVERANIMATE' IT WITH BROKEN JOINTS —
BUT MAYBE IT'S GOOD. LET'S TRY IT.

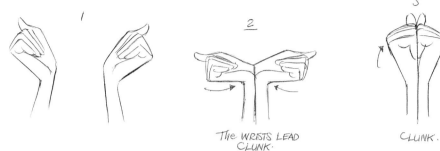

The WRISTS LEAD
CLUNK.

CLUNK.

NOW HOW ABOUT THIS FOR PULLING IT APART?

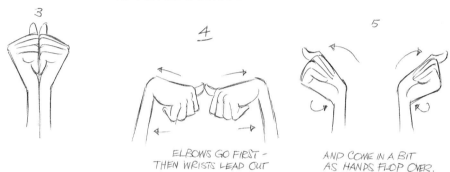

ELBOWS GO FIRST —
THEN WRISTS LEAD OUT

AND COME IN A BIT
AS HANDS FLOP OVER.

(OR) IT MIGHT BE NICE TO HAVE JUST ONE BREAK —

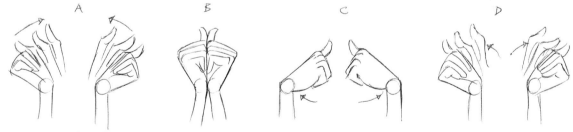

SO IT'S ALL A MATTER OF DEGREE —

WE'RE SHOWING THESE DEVICES and PRINCIPLES IN THE RAW —
IN THE CRUDEST POSSIBLE STATE TO MAKE IT CLEAR —
TO LIMBER THINGS UP — TO STOP THINGS BEING STIFF OR STILTED.

WE CAN USE THEM INCREDIBLY SUBTLY OR OVERUSE THEM
SO THINGS GO RUBBERY OR MUSHY.

BUT IT'S SURPRISING HOW FAR WE CAN GO WITH BREAKING JOINTS
and HAVE IT WORK BEAUTIFULLY.

31

FLEXIBILITY IN the FACE

THERE'S A TENDENCY TO FORGET HOW MOBILE OUR FACES REALLY ARE IN ACTION - AND IT'S ALWAYS SHOCKING TO SEE HOW MUCH DISTORTION THERE IS WHEN WE LOOK AT LIVE ACTION OF ACTORS' CLOSE-UPS FRAME BY FRAME.

NOT TO MENTION WHAT A FACIAL CONTORTIONIST CAN DO (IN SPITE OF the JAWS and TEETH NOT BEING RUBBER.)

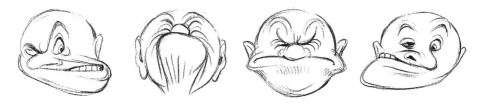

THE SKULL OBVIOUSLY REMAINS the SAME BUT THERE'S <u>LOTS</u> OF ACTION HAPPENING BELOW THE CHEEKBONES. OUR UPPER TEETH DON'T CHANGE POSITION AS THEY'RE LOCKED ONTO OUR SKULL. THE HINGED LOWER JAW ACTION IS PRIMARILY UP and DOWN WITH A SLIGHT LATERAL MOTION.

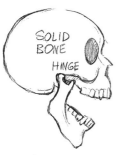

SOLID BONE

HINGE

the TENDENCY IS TO FORGET JUST HOW BIG OUR MOUTH CAVITY IS...

OUR DENTIST KNOWS HOW BIG IT IS.

the LOWER JAW IS HINGED IN FRONT OF the EAR.

AND HOW SMALL IT CAN APPEAR.

ART BABBITT OFTEN TOLD OF HOW, AFTER ANIMATING the BEAUTIFUL EVIL QUEEN 'MAGIC MIRROR ON the WALL' SCENE IN "SNOW WHITE and the SEVEN DWARFS" (A DEGREE OF REALISM THAT NO ONE HAD EVER ATTEMPTED BEFORE, LET ALONE SUCCEED IN ACHIEVING,) HE BECAME INHIBITED WHEN ANIMATING CLOSE-UPS ON the 7 DWARFS. HE GOT HELP FROM the OTHER TOP MEN IN DARING TO COMPRESS and DISTEND the FACES. HE ALWAYS SAID, "BE BRAVE. DON'T BE AFRAID TO STRETCH the FACE."

and COMPRESS IT.

THERE'S A TENDENCY TO HAVE A SIMPLE MOUTH SQUIRMING AROUND - FLOATING ON The FACE

STRETCH IT TO MAKE IT AN INTEGRAL PART OF the FACE.

THERE'S A TREMENDOUS AMOUNT OF ELASTICITY IN OUR FACE MUSCLES.

A MAN SMOKING A PIPE - (LEAVING OUT The PIPE)

SUCKING IN

PUFFING OUT

TAKE CHEWING, FOR EXAMPLE:

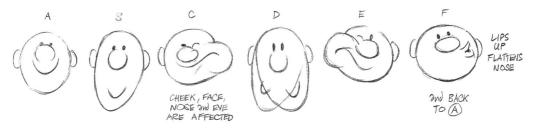

A   B   C   D   E   F

CHEEK, FACE, NOSE and EYE ARE AFFECTED

LIPS UP FLATTENS NOSE

and BACK TO (A)

WE COULD GO FROM ANY OF THESE POSITIONS TO ANY OTHER IN ANY SEQUENCE, VARYING IT.

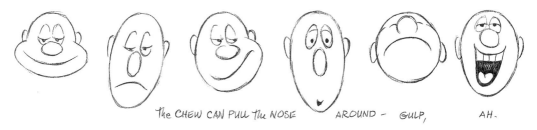

The CHEW CAN PULL The NOSE   AROUND —   GULP,   AH.

AGAIN, WITH SQUASH and STRETCH, WE TRY TO KEEP The SAME AMOUNT OF MEAT.
IF YOU TOOK IT OUT and WEIGHED IT — IT WOULD WEIGH The SAME.

AN UNCOUTH FELLOW —

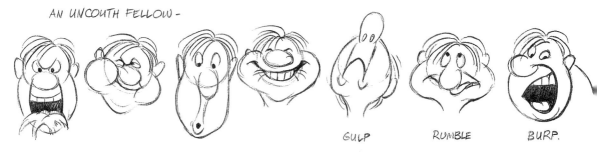

GULP   RUMBLE   BURP.

SO, AGAIN, IT'S <u>WHO</u> IS CHEWING? FAT, SMALL, OLD, CRAZY, INHIBITED?
A SOPHISTICATED PERSON CHEWING VERSUS A TRAMP WHO HASN'T EATEN FOR 3 WEEKS?

A SOCIETY MATRON NEVER OPENS HER MOUTH —

VERSUS A LABOURER EATING —

OVERLAPPING ACTION IN The FACE

HERE'S A THING YOU OFTEN SEE GOOD ACTORS DOING:
SAY SOMEONE GETS FRIGHTENED –

IT'S CRUDE
JUST TO GO

FROM ONE
TO The OTHER.

IT CAN GO IN SECTIONS –

ONE
THING
AT A
TIME –

The OVERLAPPING
ACTION WORKS
IT'S WAY
DOWN
The FACE
(CAN BE
VERY FAST)

FIRST The EYE – THEN The NOSE – THEN The MOUTH – THEN The HAIR

(OR) VICE VERSA – WORKS IT'S WAY UP The FACE –

FIRST The MOUTH – THEN The NOSE – THEN The EYE – THEN The HAIR .

START FROM SQUINT –

EYE OPENS FIRST – NOSE STRAIGHTENS – JAW FALLS   2nd OPENS

35

START WITH THE EYES — THEN KEEP GOING
AS THE MOUTH OVERLAPS and STRETCHES

(OR) THE CHANGE COULD TRAVEL ACROSS THE FACE. ←

SAY SOMEONE'S DISAPPOINTED —

START
FROM
ITS
OPPOSITE —
(THIS MIGHT
HAPPEN MORE
SLOWLY)

EYE GOES FIRST — THEN THE MOUTH   DROPS —   THE EYEBROW REVERSES   and BROW FURROWS and CHIN GOES IN.

WE ALL KNOW
THE TWO FACE —
THE
DOUBLE FACE
WHERE
THERE'S
CONTRADICTION:

 PLUS  EQUALS =

PUTTING
A BRAVE
FACE ON IT —

ONE SIDE OF THE FACE IS TELLING US ONE THING and THE OTHER SIDE IS TELLING US ANOTHER —

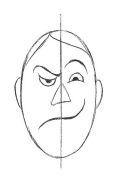   

I'D LIKE TO ANIMATE ONE SIDE SEPARATELY and THEN ANIMATE THE OTHER.

36

THIS HAS TO GO IN the BOOK SOMEWHERE and IT MIGHT AS WELL BE HERE...

WHAT'S THIS?

OR THIS?

BUT IT'S PRETTY CLEAR WHAT THIS → IS.

IF WE WANT OUR AUDIENCE TO READ AN ACTION FAST - SHOW IT IN PROFILE.

NOT → BUT →

AND NOT → BUT

AND NOT → BUT →

WE CERTAINLY DON'T HAVE ANY TROUBLE SEEING WHAT'S HAPPENING HERE—

Ⓐ Ⓑ Ⓒ Ⓓ Ⓔ Ⓕ Ⓖ

AND FROM the POINT OF VIEW OF FLEXIBILITY - LOOK HOW JUST A SIMPLE REVERSAL OF HER BACK ARCH GIVES TERRIFIC SUPPLENESS. DRAWING Ⓓ'S BACK IS ABOUT AS CONCAVE AS YOU CAN GET - STAYS THAT WAY ON Ⓔ and THEN REVERSES TO CONVEX ON Ⓕ and Ⓖ. The HAIR IS DELAYED and ONLY DROPS ON Ⓕ. NICE.

IT'S ALWAYS A GOOD IDEA TO TRY TO GET A CLEAR OPPOSITE FROM WHAT WE'RE GOING TO CHANGE TO - WHETHER IT'S A FACIAL EXPRESSION OR A CHANGE OF SHAPE LIKE THIS.

TO FINISH OFF THIS SECTION and AS A KIND OF REVIEW -

HERE'S AN EXAM IN FLEXIBILITY -

AN ASSIGNMENT ART BABBITT GAVE US TO PRACTICE SUCCESSIVE BREAKING JOINTS -

(1) TAKE THE FRONT VIEW OF A FEMALE SWAYING SIDE TO SIDE.
(2) HAVE THE HIPS WORK IN A FIGURE 8.
(3) HAVE THE HEAD COUNTER THE BODY.
(4) HAVE THE HANDS WORK INDEPENDENTLY and BREAK THE JOINTS.

HERE'S THE SCRIBBLE I MADE AS ART SET OUT THE PROBLEM:

HIPS
WORK
IN FIGURE 8

KIND OF A SCARY PROBLEM and AS I WANTED TO DO IT SORT OF REALISTICALLY - EVEN SCARIER.
OK, WHAT DO WE DO FIRST? (THINKS) DUHHH... HEY, OF COURSE - THE (KEY) = DRAWING #(1)
THE ONE THAT TELLS THE STORY

(1)

13

WHAT'S NEXT?
(THINKS)
... OBVIOUSLY...
THE NEXT EXTREME
WHERE SHE'LL SWAY
TO THE OTHER SIDE

- CALL THIS #13
BECAUSE WHEN
I ACT IT OUT
I TAKE ABOUT
½ A SECOND TO SWING
TO ONE SIDE and
½ SEC. TO SWING BACK
= 1 SECOND OVERALL.

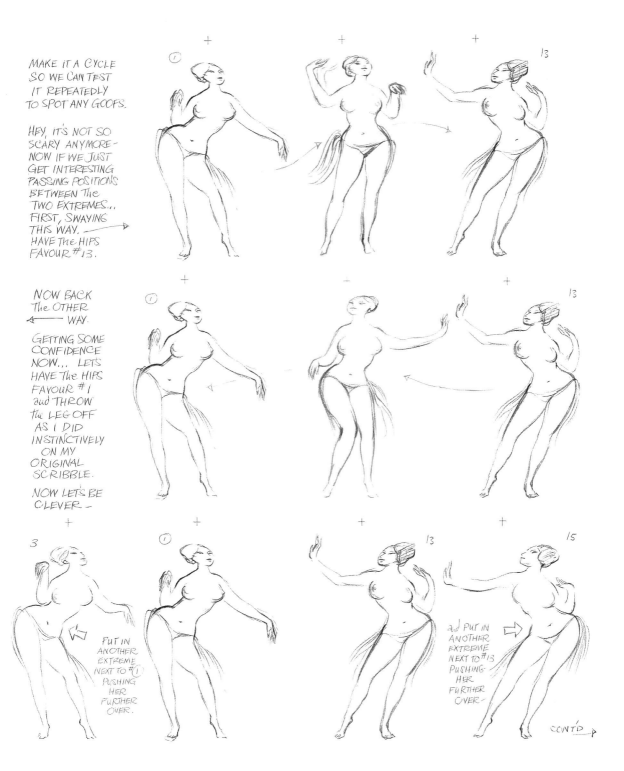

MAKE IT A CYCLE
SO WE CAN TEST
IT REPEATEDLY
TO SPOT ANY GOOFS.

HEY, IT'S NOT SO
SCARY ANYMORE—
NOW IF WE JUST
GET INTERESTING
PASSING POSITIONS
BETWEEN THE
TWO EXTREMES...
FIRST, SWAYING
THIS WAY.
HAVE THE HIPS
FAVOUR #13.

NOW BACK
THE OTHER
WAY.

GETTING SOME
CONFIDENCE
NOW... LET'S
HAVE THE HIPS
FAVOUR #1
and THROW
THE LEG OFF
AS I DID
INSTINCTIVELY
ON MY
ORIGINAL
SCRIBBLE.

NOW LET'S BE
CLEVER—

PUT IN
ANOTHER
EXTREME
NEXT TO #1
PUSHING
HER
FURTHER
OVER.

and PUT IN
ANOTHER
EXTREME
NEXT TO #13
PUSHING·
HER
FURTHER
OVER—

CONT'D ▶

39

NOW IT LOOKS
LIKE IT'S ALL
GOING TO WORK~

and WE CAN
KIND OF RELAX,
BREAKING IT DOWN
FURTHER
and ENJOY TAKING
ON The REST
BIT BY BIT~
PUTTING IN The
HANDS CIRCLING
and OTHER
CURVY BITS.

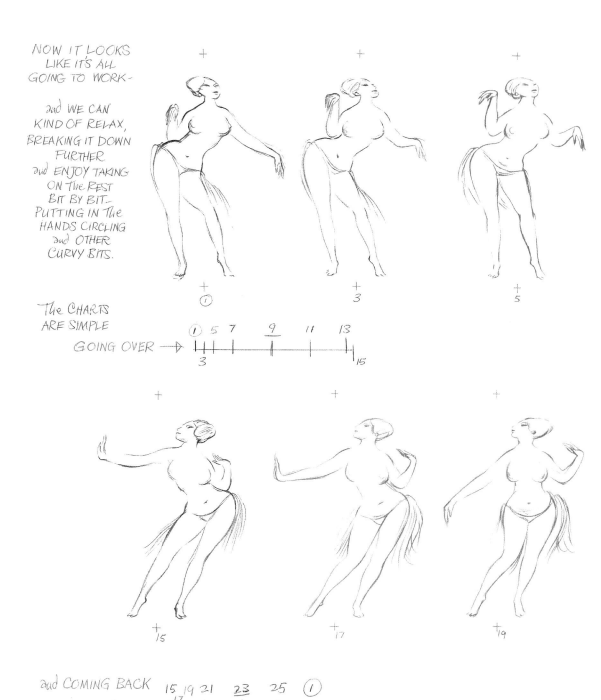

The CHARTS
ARE SIMPLE

GOING OVER ⟶ ▷

①   5   7   9   11   13

3   15

and COMING BACK   15 19 21   23   25   ①

17

◁

40

7   9   11   13

21   23   25   1

THEN ADD IN ONES THROUGHOUT — BUT THEY'RE JUST BRAINLESS IN BETWEENS TO SMOOTH THINGS OUT FURTHER. (THIS CAME OUT JUST FINE, DIDN'T NEED ANY CORRECTIONS.)

41

SOMEHOW I LEFT THIS OUT OF THE 1ST EDITION —

IT'S REALLY ("LESSON ONE" ON FLEXIBILITY)

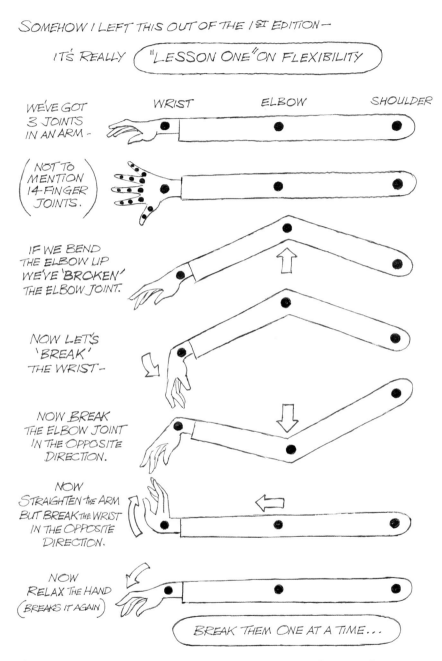

WE'VE GOT 3 JOINTS IN AN ARM —

WRIST   ELBOW   SHOULDER

(NOT TO MENTION 14-FINGER JOINTS.)

IF WE BEND THE ELBOW UP WE'VE 'BROKEN' THE ELBOW JOINT.

NOW LET'S 'BREAK' THE WRIST —

NOW BREAK THE ELBOW JOINT IN THE OPPOSITE DIRECTION.

NOW STRAIGHTEN the ARM BUT BREAK the WRIST IN THE OPPOSITE DIRECTION.

NOW RELAX the HAND (BREAKS IT AGAIN)

(BREAK THEM ONE AT A TIME...)

IF ALL THE JOINTS DO NOT BREAK AT THE SAME TIME, WE CAN ACHIEVE ALL THE FLUIDITY AND FLEXIBILITY WE'LL EVER NEED IN ANIMATION!

THIS WAS A VERY BIG LESSON FOR ME!

YEARS AGO ONE OF MY BETTER EFFORTS WAS A SCENE OF A WITCH SAYING,
"I'M GOING TO GIVE YOU THE ELIXIR." I HAD HER HANDS WORKING BACKWARDS
AND FORWARDS LIKE AN ITALIAN WAITER. (I'M JUST SHOWING RANDOM DRAWINGS HERE)

PLEASED WITH IT, I RAN IT FOR ART BABBITT, WHO GRUNTED, "WELL, OK,
BUT YOU'RE 'TWINNING' THE HANDS. HOW MUCH BETTER IT WOULD BE IF YOU
WERE TO DELAY JUST ONE OF HER HANDS FOR 4 FRAMES. TO BREAK IT UP."
I DID IT. THE REST OF THE FIGURE WAS THE SAME - BUT THE DELAYED HAND MADE IT!
(AGAIN - JUST RANDOM DRAWINGS HERE)

LEFT HAND
ARRIVES
4 FRAMES LATE

DELIGHTED WITH THE RESULT, I PROUDLY RAN IT FOR KEN HARRIS.
"YEAH, ALRIGHT," KEN GROWLED, "BUT WHY DIDN'T YOU PROGRESS THE ACTION?
MOVE HER FORWARD AS SHE GESTURES." (SEE 'THE SECRET' OF LIP SYNC ON PAGE 314.)
SO I DREW THE WHOLE THING ALL OVER AGAIN, 'PROGRESSING' HER. THE ACTION
WAS EXACTLY THE SAME BUT I MOVED HER ACROSS THE PAGE - GOING SOMEWHERE.
THE WHOLE THING WAS TRANSFORMED. (THIS IS THE BEST I CAN DO TO SHOW IT HERE.)

SAME DRAWINGS (RETRACED) PROGRESSING HER FORWARD ACROSS THE PAGE -

WEIGHT

THE FIRST QUESTION I EVER ASKED MILT KAHL WAS: 'HOW DID YOU EVER GET THAT JUNGLE BOOK TIGER TO WEIGH SO MUCH?'

HE ANSWERED, 'WELL, I KNOW WHERE the WEIGHT IS ON EVERY DRAWING. I KNOW WHERE the WEIGHT IS AT ANY GIVEN MOMENT ON the CHARACTER. I KNOW WHERE the WEIGHT IS, and WHERE IT'S COMING FROM and WHERE IT'S JUST TRAVELLING OVER - and WHERE the WEIGHT IS TRANSFERRING TO.'

WE'VE ALREADY SEEN THAT IN A WALK WE FEEL the WEIGHT ON the DOWN POSITION WHERE the LEG BENDS AS IT TAKES the WEIGHT, ABSORBING the FORCE OF the MOVE. BUT HOW ABOUT OTHER KINDS OF WEIGHT? OBJECTS - LIGHT? HEAVY? HOW DO WE SHOW THAT?

ONE WAY WE CAN SHOW HOW HEAVY AN OBJECT IS -
- IS BY the WAY WE PREPARE TO PICK IT UP.
TO PICK UP WEIGHT WE HAVE TO PREPARE FOR IT - TO ANTICIPATE the WEIGHT. OBVIOUSLY PICKING UP A PIECE OF CHALK, A PEN OR A FEATHER DOESN'T REQUIRE ANY PREPARATION -

BUT A HEAVY STONE...

WE CAN SUGGEST WEIGHT BY JUST HAVING HIM WALK AROUND IT - SIZING IT UP.

BAD. NO FEELING OF WEIGHT.
IT MUST BE A POLYSTYRENE ROCK.

HOW'S HE GOING TO DO THIS? HE'S CONSIDERING WHAT HE'S GOING TO PICK UP. HOW HEAVY IS IT? HE'S ANTICIPATING WHAT IT'S GOING TO WEIGH...

44

MAYBE WE DON'T HAVE The SCREEN TIME TO HAVE HIM WALK AROUND, BUT ONE WAY OR ANOTHER, HE'S GOING TO ANTICIPATE The WEIGHT.

LOOK WHAT THE SPINE IS DOING...

HE'D CERTAINLY SPREAD HIS FEET FIRST AND BEND HIS KNEES.

AND GET AS CLOSE TO The WEIGHT AS POSSIBLE.

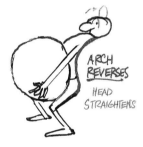

ARCH REVERSES

HEAD STRAIGHTENS

HE ADJUSTS HIMSELF SO AS TO NOT DAMAGE HIMSELF, HE DOESN'T WANT A HERNIA.

BODY GOES BACK AS HE LIFTS

TRIES TO GET UNDERNEATH The WEIGHT - MIGHT ADJUST FEET IN LITTLE BITS - ERRATICALLY

BACK ARCH REVERSES AS HE TRIES TO GET A PURCHASE -

ARCH TIGHTENS

ARCH STRAIGHTENS

BIG LIFT

STRAIGHTENS - KNEES SHAKE

FALLS BACK OR WHATEVER,

45

A MAN CARRYING A SACK OF POTATOES ON HIS BACK BENDS DOWN TO COUNTERBALANCE The WEIGHT.
THE WEIGHT FORCES HIS BODY CLOSER TO THE GROUND, KEEPING The KNEES BENT and MAKING The FEET
SHUFFLE ALONG. The FEET ALSO SPLAY OUT TO FORM A SORT OF TRIPOD TO SPREAD The WEIGHT OVER
A LARGER AREA.

FEET APART-
KNEES
ALWAYS BENT

FEET DON'T
COME OFF
The GROUND
VERY MUCH.

A LOT OF DIFFERENCE IN THESE WALKS OR RUNS IS DETERMINED BY The WEIGHT The PERSON MIGHT BE CARRYING.
IF A PERSON IS CARRYING A HEAVY ROCK-
The WEIGHT WOULD LOWER The SHOULDERS and STRETCH The ARMS. The HEAD and NECK COULD COME DOWN.

(PULLED SLIGHTLY APART)   17   9   1

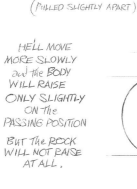

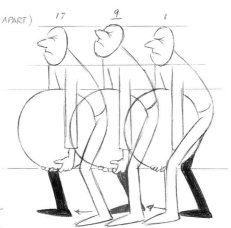

HE'LL MOVE
MORE SLOWLY
and the BODY
WILL RAISE
ONLY SLIGHTLY
ON The
PASSING POSITION

BUT The ROCK
WILL NOT RAISE
AT ALL.

AGAIN The
PASSING FOOT
WILL HARDLY
LEAVE The GROUND
and
The KNEES WILL
REMAIN BENT
ALL The TIME
FROM The WEIGHT.

The TIMING OF The FEET
COULD BE ERRATIC -

i.e. STEP, PAUSE, STEP, STEP, PAUSE, STEP, PAUSE, STEP, STEP, STEP, PAUSE, etc.
OR HE COULD GLIDE RAPIDLY and THEN DROP IT.

46

A HAND PICKING UP A SILK
HANDKERCHIEF LYING ON
THE GROUND ENCOUNTERS
NO RESISTANCE –

BUT A HAND PICKING UP A BRICK –
LET'S CONSIDER WHAT HAPPENS TO THE WHOLE BODY –

ANGLE OF HEAD
COULD OPPOSE
SHOULDERS.

THE WEIGHT
OF THE BRICK
STRAIGHTENS
THE ARM
and PULLS
THE SHOULDER
DOWN.

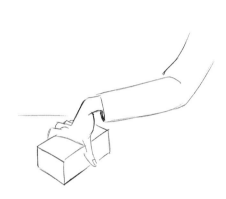 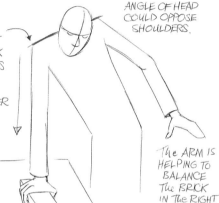

THE ARM IS
HELPING TO
BALANCE
THE BRICK
IN THE RIGHT
HAND.

PICKING UP A FEATHER
ISN'T GOING TO HAVE ANY EFFECT ON THE BODY.

 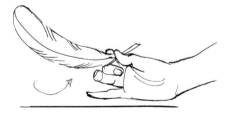

REVERSING THE FEATHER SHAPE TO ‿ IN THE MOVE MAKES THE FEATHER EVEN
LIGHTER.

OF COURSE, ONE WAY TO GET WEIGHT IS TO BE CONSCIOUS OF IT.

THE GREAT ANIMATOR, BILL TYTLA SAYS –

"THE POINT IS THAT YOU ARE NOT MERELY SWISHING A PENCIL ABOUT, BUT YOU HAVE
WEIGHT IN YOUR FORMS and YOU DO WHATEVER YOU POSSIBLY CAN WITH THAT WEIGHT
TO CONVEY SENSATION. IT IS A STRUGGLE FOR ME and I AM CONSCIOUS OF IT ALL THE TIME."

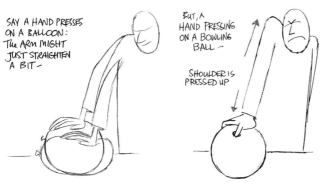

SAY A HAND PRESSES ON A BALLOON: THE ARM MIGHT JUST STRAIGHTEN A BIT —

BUT, A HAND PRESSING ON A BOWLING BALL —

SHOULDER IS PRESSED UP

A HAND PRESSING ON WATER

THE HAND WILL DISPLACE SOME OF THE WATER BUT WILL REALLY HAVE LITTLE EFFECT ON THE WATER.

LET'S DROP A FEW THINGS WHICH FALL AT DIFFERENT SPEEDS BECAUSE OF THEIR WEIGHT and WHAT THEY'RE MADE OF.

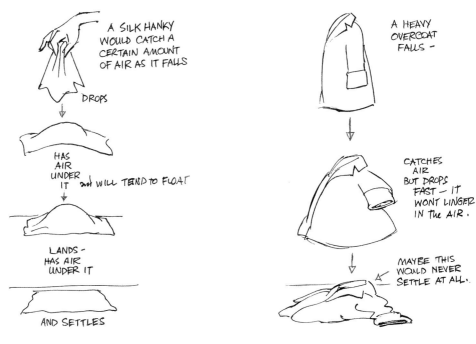

A SILK HANKY WOULD CATCH A CERTAIN AMOUNT OF AIR AS IT FALLS

DROPS

HAS AIR UNDER IT and WILL TEND TO FLOAT

LANDS — HAS AIR UNDER IT

AND SETTLES

A HEAVY OVERCOAT FALLS —

CATCHES AIR BUT DROPS FAST — IT WON'T LINGER IN THE AIR.

MAYBE THIS WOULD NEVER SETTLE AT ALL.

TAKE A CHINA CUP —

IN REALITY THE CUP WOULD PROBABLY SHATTER ON IMPACT BUT WE CAN HAVE IT BOUNCE AROUND A BIT. TAKE LIBERTIES WITH REALITY BUT MAKE IT APPEAR BELIEVABLE.

BOUNCE.   BOUNCE.   BOUNCE.   BOUNCE.   SETTLES   PAUSE    THEN IT SHATTERS.

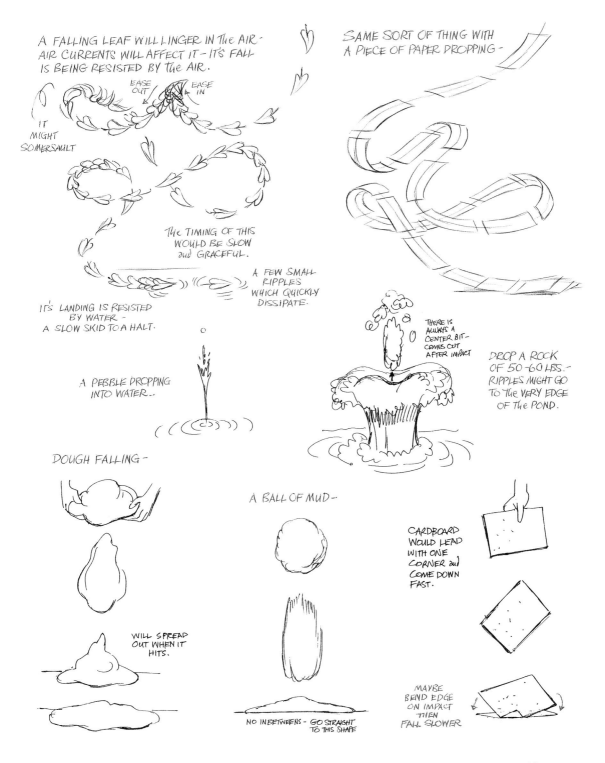

A FALLING LEAF WILL LINGER IN THE AIR - AIR CURRENTS WILL AFFECT IT - IT'S FALL IS BEING RESISTED BY THE AIR.

EASE OUT
EASE IN

IT MIGHT SOMERSAULT

THE TIMING OF THIS WOULD BE SLOW and GRACEFUL.

A FEW SMALL RIPPLES WHICH QUICKLY DISSIPATE.

IT'S LANDING IS RESISTED BY WATER - A SLOW SKID TO A HALT.

SAME SORT OF THING WITH A PIECE OF PAPER DROPPING -

A PEBBLE DROPPING INTO WATER..

THERE IS ALWAYS A CENTER BIT - COMES OUT AFTER IMPACT

DROP A ROCK OF 50-60 LBS. - RIPPLES MIGHT GO TO THE VERY EDGE OF THE POND.

DOUGH FALLING -

A BALL OF MUD -

WILL SPREAD OUT WHEN IT HITS.

NO INBETWEENS - GO STRAIGHT TO THIS SHAPE

CARDBOARD WOULD LEAD WITH ONE CORNER and COME DOWN FAST.

MAYBE BEND EDGE ON IMPACT THEN FALL SLOWER

49

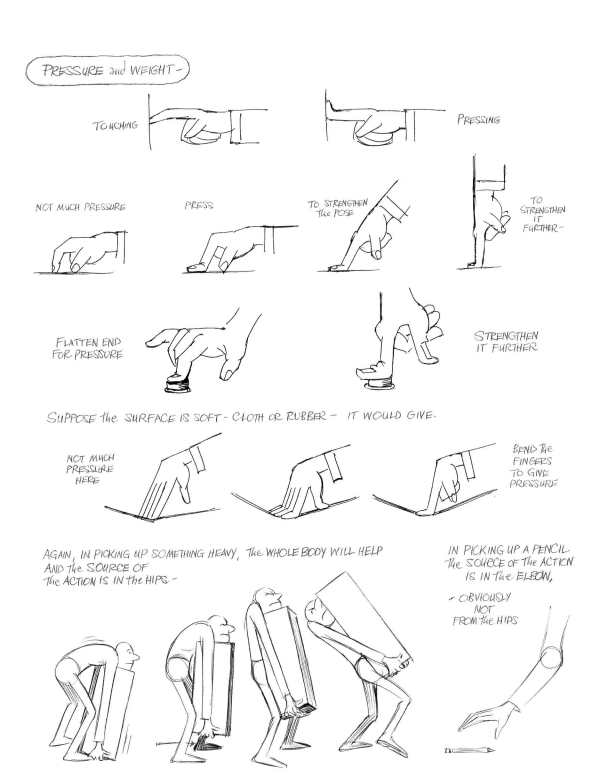

PRESSURE and WEIGHT —

TOUCHING

PRESSING

NOT MUCH PRESSURE

PRESS

TO STRENGTHEN THE POSE

TO STRENGTHEN IT FURTHER —

FLATTEN END FOR PRESSURE

STRENGTHEN IT FURTHER

SUPPOSE the SURFACE IS SOFT — CLOTH OR RUBBER — IT WOULD GIVE.

NOT MUCH PRESSURE HERE

BEND the FINGERS TO GIVE PRESSURE

AGAIN, IN PICKING UP SOMETHING HEAVY, The WHOLE BODY WILL HELP AND the SOURCE OF The ACTION IS IN the HIPS —

IN PICKING UP A PENCIL The SOURCE OF The ACTION IS IN The ELBOW,

— OBVIOUSLY NOT FROM the HIPS

50

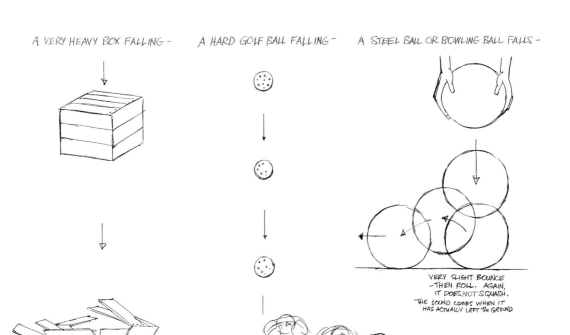

A VERY HEAVY BOX FALLING -   A HARD GOLF BALL FALLING-   A STEEL BALL OR BOWLING BALL FALLS -

VERY SLIGHT BOUNCE
-THEN ROLL. AGAIN,
IT DOES NOT SQUASH.

THE SOUND COMES WHEN IT
HAS ACTUALLY LEFT the GROUND

TO FEEL the IMPACT The BOX IS PARTIALLY OPEN
AT The MOMENT OF IMPACT.

WHEN IT HITS WE
SHOW the CONTACT
BUT IT DOES NOT SQUASH
AND IMMEDIATELY RISES.

IT BOUNCES BUT IMMEDIATELY ROLLS TO A STOP.

ROLLS → STOPS

A TENNIS BALL WILL SQUASH ON IMPACT

THEN
REGAIN ITS
ORIGINAL
SHAPE

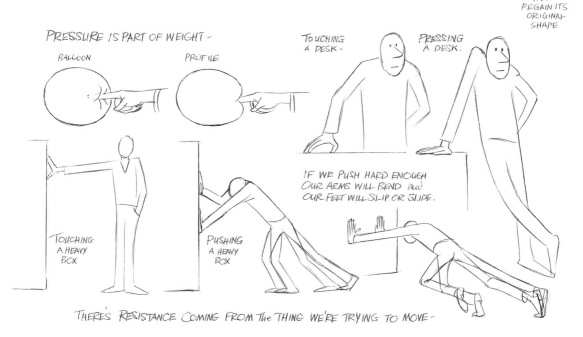

PRESSURE IS PART OF WEIGHT -

BALLOON   PROFILE   TOUCHING A DESK -   PRESSING A DESK.

!IF WE PUSH HARD ENOUGH
OUR ARMS WILL BEND and
OUR FEET WILL SLIP OR SLIDE.

TOUCHING
A HEAVY
BOX

PUSHING
A HEAVY
BOX

THERE'S RESISTANCE COMING FROM The THING WE'RE TRYING TO MOVE-

51

> HOW MUCH EFFORT DO WE HAVE TO EXPEND
> ① TO MOVE SOMETHING?
> ② TO CHANGE ITS DIRECTION?
> ③ OR TO STOP IT?
> WILL INDICATE HOW MUCH IT WEIGHS.

COMING TO A STOP IS PART OF WEIGHT:

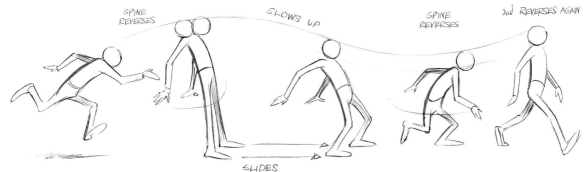

SPINE REVERSES

SLOWS UP

SPINE REVERSES

2nd REVERSES AGAIN

SLIDES

COMING TO the END OF A SLIDE, WE'RE THROWN OFF BALANCE

THEN WE GO INTO OUR NEXT ACTION – LIKE COMING OFF AN ESCALATOR.

FRANK THOMAS SAYS –
"WE'VE GOT TO DO SOMETHING TO STOP The FORWARD PROGRESSION OF BELIEVABLE WEIGHT."

WHATEVER WAS IN MOTION WILL TRY TO KEEP ON GOING –

ARMS, HEAD, HANDS, HAIR, DRAPERY.

SO WE STOP IN BITS – EACH BIT INDICATING the WEIGHT OF ITSELF.

HERE'S MILT KAHL ON IT –
"STOPPING THINGS CONVINCINGLY IS ONE OF The DIFFICULT THINGS TO DO IN ANIMATION. WHEN YOU COME TO A STOP, PICK A GOOD PLACE TO STOP. HOW YOU CHOOSE TO STOP – WHAT KIND OF A STOP – WHETHER IT'S AN ALERT STOP OR A LAZY ONE, CHOOSING WHERE TO DO IT IS AN IMPORTANT CHOICE. I HATE TO SEE A FOOT COME THROUGH 2nd LAND 2nd THEN NOTHING HAPPENS TO IT. I THINK WHEN IT LANDS WE OUGHT TO GO AHEAD 2nd PUT The WEIGHT ON IT – OR ROCK FORWARD – OR RAISE THE OTHER FOOT."

SO, HOW MUCH EFFORT IT TAKES TO STOP SOMETHING SHOWS HOW MUCH IT WEIGHS.

ALSO, THE SPEED OF AN ACTION WILL DETERMINE HOW VIOLENT THE DRAPERY IS —

IF A MAN IS RUNNING WITH A COAT MADE OF THIN, LIGHT MATERIAL AND HE COMES TO A SUDDEN STOP, THE MATERIAL WILL CONTINUE TO FLOW, TO KEEP ON GOING — TO GO AHEAD OF HIM INDEPENDENTLY AND THEN FLOP BACK AND SETTLE. ('FOLLOWS THROUGH')

STOPS — MATERIAL CONTINUES   AND SETTLES

A WOMAN IN A SILK NIGHTIE... THE MATERIAL WILL BLOSSOM AND FLAP VIOLENTLY.

STOPS — MATERIAL CONTINUES   AND WILL SETTLE MORE
BLOSSOMING   SLOWLY.

SO WHEN SHE STOPS, HER CLOTHES AND HAIR FOLLOW THROUGH ARRIVING LATER THAN THE MAIN ACTION. AND OF COURSE, HER MAIN ACTION ALSO STOPS IN PARTS, FINISHING UP AT DIFFERENT TIMES.

HAS THERE EVER BEEN AN ACTION WHERE ALL THE PARTS OF A BODY MOVED UNIFORMLY? (EXCEPT IN ROBOTS, AND PROBABLY NOT EVEN IN THEM.)

AGAIN, 'FOLLOW THROUGH' IS THE RESULT OF AND IS GENERATED BY THE MAIN ACTION.

BUT the ONLY WAY WE CAN REALLY SHOW WEIGHT IS WITH the ACTION.
SAY WE'RE PICKING UP A HEAVY BATCH OF HAY WITH A PITCHFORK—

ANTICIPATES
THRUST

BACK ARCH
REVERSES

DIGS IN FAST

IT'S SLOW LIFTING —

DELAY
HEAD

BACK
ARCH
REVERSES
AGAIN

IT JERKS UP
BREAKING FREE

ANTICIPATES the THROW
BY GOING DOWN —

BACK
ARCH
REVERSES
AGAIN

BACK
ARCH
REVERSES
AGAIN!

NOW
I'M ABLE TO
THROW IT —

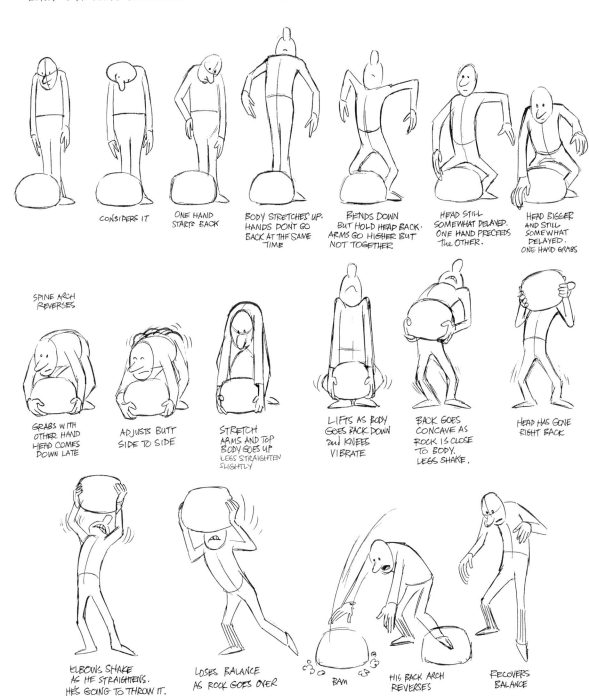

CONSIDERS IT

ONE HAND
STARTS BACK

BODY STRETCHES UP.
HANDS DON'T GO
BACK AT THE SAME
TIME

BENDS DOWN
BUT HOLD HEAD BACK.
ARMS GO HIGHER BUT
NOT TOGETHER

HEAD STILL
SOMEWHAT DELAYED.
ONE HAND PRECEDS
The OTHER.

HEAD BIGGER
AND STILL
SOMEWHAT
DELAYED.
ONE HAND GRABS

SPINE ARCH
REVERSES

GRABS WITH
OTHER HAND
HEAD COMES
DOWN LATE

ADJUSTS BUTT
SIDE TO SIDE

STRETCH
ARMS AND TOP
BODY GOES UP
LEGS STRAIGHTEN
SLIGHTLY

LIFTS AS BODY
GOES BACK DOWN
2nd KNEES
VIBRATE

BACK GOES
CONCAVE AS
ROCK IS CLOSE
TO BODY.
LEGS SHAKE.

HEAD HAS GONE
RIGHT BACK

ELBOWS SHAKE
AS HE STRAIGHTENS.
HE'S GOING TO THROW IT.

LOSES BALANCE
AS ROCK GOES OVER

BAM

HIS BACK ARCH
REVERSES

RECOVERS
BALANCE

55

A MAN WITH A HEAVY MALLET IS GOING TO THROW IT ON AN ANVIL—

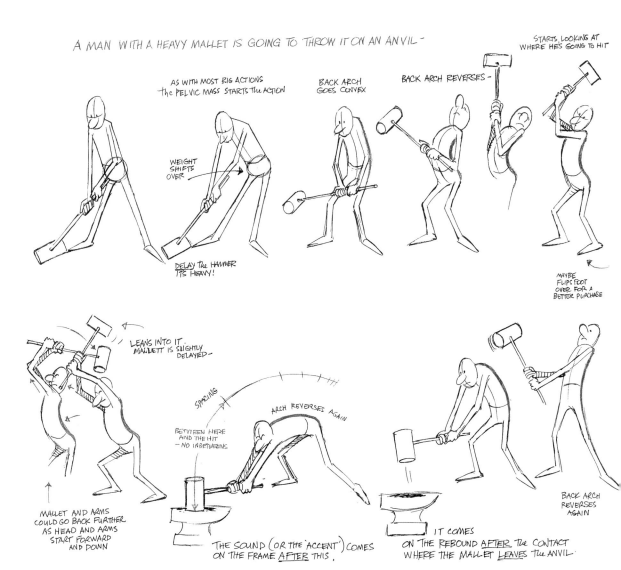

AS WITH MOST BIG ACTIONS the PELVIC MASS STARTS the ACTION

BACK ARCH GOES CONVEX

BACK ARCH REVERSES—

STARTS, LOOKING AT WHERE HE'S GOING TO HIT

WEIGHT SHIFTS OVER

DELAY The HAMMER ITS HEAVY!

MAYBE FLIPS FOOT OVER FOR A BETTER PURCHASE

LEANS INTO IT. MALLETT IS SLIGHTLY DELAYED—

MALLET AND ARMS COULD GO BACK FURTHER AS HEAD AND ARMS START FORWARD AND DOWN

SPACING

BETWEEN HERE AND THE HIT — NO INBETWEENS

ARCH REVERSES AGAIN

THE SOUND (OR THE 'ACCENT') COMES ON THE FRAME AFTER THIS.

BACK ARCH REVERSES AGAIN

IT COMES ON THE REBOUND AFTER The CONTACT WHERE THE MALLET LEAVES The ANVIL.

SO WE TRY TO FIND ALL The VARIOUS POSSIBILITIES TO CONVEY WEIGHT VISUALLY—

CAN WE DELAY PARTS?
GO FAST AND SLOW?
USE UP AND DOWN?
BREAK The JOINTS?
REVERSE The BODY ARCH?
SHIFT The WEIGHT?

— AND SELECT WHAT WE NEED TO PUT OVER WHAT WE WANT.
AND WHEN WE HAVE ALL THIS STUFF IN OUR BLOODSTREAM — CONCENTRATE ON PERSONALITY.
WHO IS DOING IT and IN WHAT SITUATION?

RUNNING and TRYING TO CHANGE DIRECTION SHOWS the WEIGHT.

IN TURNING A CORNER CHARLIE CHAPLIN DID A FAMOUS SKIDDING OR HOPPING TURN.
HE SKIDS ROUND the CORNER IN A CURVE and RUNS OUT the OTHER WAY.

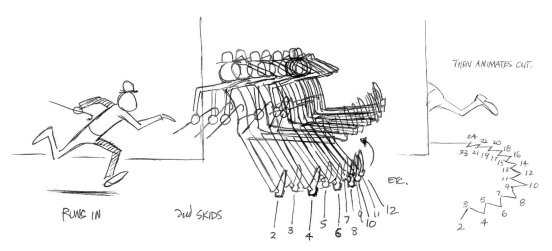

RUNS IN   and SKIDS   THEN ANIMATES OUT.   ETC.

LIKE A MOTORBIKE HE LEANS INTO the CURVE OF the TURN.

IN ANIMATION - IF HE SKIDS FOR ABOUT A SECOND -
A WAY TO DO THIS IS TO MAKE A SERIES OF DRAWINGS FROM 2 TO 24 (EVEN NUMBERS)
THEN MAKE ANOTHER SERIES, OFFSET SLIGHTLY, FROM 3 to 23 (ODD NUMBERS)
THEN WE INTERLEAVE THEM. (FOR MORE ON THIS SEE 'VIBRATIONS')

THE FEET ARE OFFSET ON The
IN BETWEENS TO MAKE The SKID.

DANCING

        TO FINISH OFF THIS SECTION ON WEIGHT WE SHOULD INCLUDE DANCING.
The REASON IS THAT the ESSENTIAL PART OF DANCING IS NOT WHAT'S HAPPENING TO the FEET
BUT WHAT'S HAPPENING TO THE BODY - the WEIGHT - the UP and DOWN OF the BODY.

KEN HARRIS and ART BABBITT WERE BOTH SPECIALISTS IN DANCE ANIMATION and THEY
BOTH SAID EXACTLY the SAME THING: IT'S the UP AND DOWN ON the BODY and HANDS
THAT IS the MOST IMPORTANT THING IN A DANCE. IT'S WHAT'S HAPPENING TO the BODY
                WITH the WEIGHT MOVING UP and DOWN IN RHYTHM.

IN A TAP DANCE-   (PULLED APART)

IF WE BLOCK OUT the FEET and JUST GET the UP and DOWN OF the BODY RIGHT-
        THEN WE CAN PUT the FEET ON ANYWHERE.

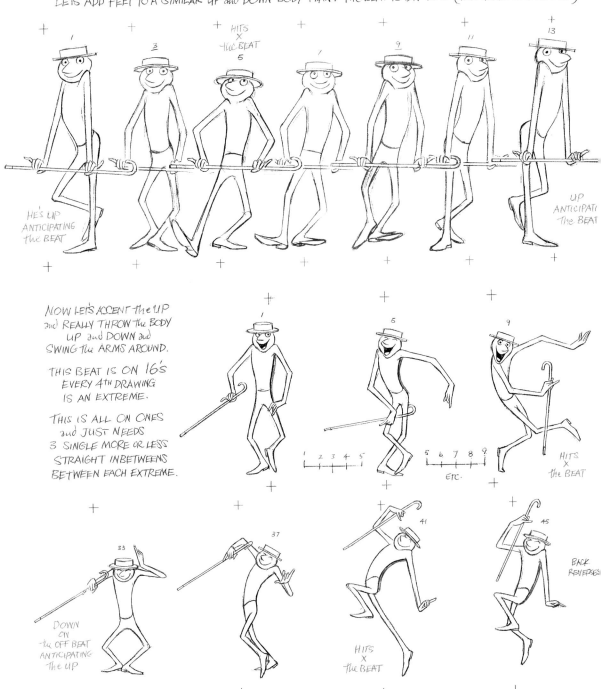

LET'S ADD FEET TO A SIMILAR UP and DOWN BODY PLAN. THE BEAT IS ON 12'S (THIS WORKS WELL ON TWOS)

HE'S UP
ANTICIPATING
THE BEAT

HITS
X
THE BEAT
5

UP
ANTICIPATI
THE BEAT

NOW LET'S ACCENT THE UP
and REALLY THROW THE BODY
UP and DOWN and
SWING THE ARMS AROUND.

THIS BEAT IS ON 16'S
EVERY 4TH DRAWING
IS AN EXTREME.

THIS IS ALL ON ONES
and JUST NEEDS
3 SINGLE MORE OR LESS
STRAIGHT INBETWEENS
BETWEEN EACH EXTREME.

HITS
X
THE BEAT

DOWN
ON
THE OFF BEAT
ANTICIPATING
THE UP

HITS
X
THE BEAT

BACK
REVERSES

58

ON A DANCE - USUALLY HIT the BEAT ON the DOWN. WE FEEL the WEIGHT AS the BODY COMES DOWN.

HITS
X
the BEAT

15   17   19   21   23   25

UP TO
ANTICIPATE

13   17   21   25   29

BACK
REVERSES -

DOWN
ON THE
OFF
BEAT

BACK
REVERSES

HITS
X
the BEAT

49   53   57

DOWN
ON the
OFF BEAT
TO GO UP

BACK
REVERSES -

HITS
X
the BEAT

WE CAN ACCENT EITHER
the DOWN OR The UP
OF the BODY.

ON A DANCE, IF WE GET MOST
OF the BIG BEATS RIGHT -
THEN WE CAN ALMOST IGNORE
The LITTLE BEATS OR SECONDARY ONES.

DONT SPEND TIME
ON THE INFINITESMAL -
ANYTHING LESS THAN
4 FRAMES WONT READ.

GET the MAIN THING RIGHT - REALLY RIGHT.
THEN SUPPORT IT WITH SECONDARY RUNS ON
STUFF.

59

WITH DANCERS - NOTICE THE TWIST IN THE SHOULDERS
AS THEY OPPOSE THE TWIST IN THE HIPS.

THE HIPS and SHOULDERS
TEND TO COUNTER EACH
OTHER ALL THE TIME -
SHOULDER DOWN, HIP UP,
SHOULDER UP, HIP DOWN.
TWIST THE BODY -
HEAD AT DIFFERENT ANGLE
TO SHOULDERS.

WHEN CHANGING
POSITION
LEAD WITH
THE HIPS
as the
WEIGHT
SHIFTS

FEET CAN COME DOWN
ON THE SIDE OF THE FOOT
THEN
STRAIGHTEN
OUT

IN
SOME STEPS
THE FEET BARELY
TOUCH THE GROUND

GET
LEAN
INTO THE BODY
FOR DYNAMICS

ON SYNCHRONISING THE ACTION TO A MUSICAL BEAT, THERE ARE 2 RULES OF THUMB:

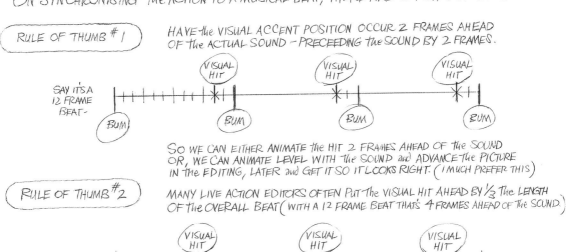

RULE OF THUMB #1   HAVE THE VISUAL ACCENT POSITION OCCUR 2 FRAMES AHEAD
OF THE ACTUAL SOUND - PRECEEDING THE SOUND BY 2 FRAMES.

SAY IT'S A
12 FRAME
BEAT -

VISUAL HIT   VISUAL HIT   VISUAL HIT
BUM   BUM   BUM   BUM

SO WE CAN EITHER ANIMATE THE HIT 2 FRAMES AHEAD OF THE SOUND
OR, WE CAN ANIMATE LEVEL WITH THE SOUND and ADVANCE THE PICTURE
IN THE EDITING, LATER and GET IT SO IT LOOKS RIGHT. (I MUCH PREFER THIS)

RULE OF THUMB #2   MANY LIVE ACTION EDITORS OFTEN PUT THE VISUAL HIT AHEAD BY 1/3 THE LENGTH
OF THE OVERALL BEAT (WITH A 12 FRAME BEAT THAT'S 4 FRAMES AHEAD OF THE SOUND.)

12 FRAME
BEAT

VISUAL HIT   VISUAL HIT   VISUAL HIT
BUM   BUM   BUM   BUM

AS WITH DIALOGUE, I THINK THE BEST WAY IS TO ANIMATE LEVEL WITH THE SOUND - THEN FIDDLE
WITH IT IN THE EDITING TILL IT LOOKS JUST RIGHT. ALSO WE LEARN THINGS THIS WAY, AS RULES
OF THUMB ARE ONLY WHAT THEY ARE - RULES OF THUMB. TRY IT and SEE WHAT WORKS BEST.
MAYBE IT'S BETTER ONE FRAME ADVANCED, MAYBE TWO, MAYBE 3 OR 4. MAYBE ITS BEST LEVEL.
(IT'S NEVER BETTER LATE.)